Presented to:

_____

From:

_____

Date:

_____

"In *God's Weapons of War*, Dr. Hamon issues a prophetic call for believers to step fully into their role in God's army. We are to be soldiers who walk in purity and power, abiding in the Lord, so that heaven and earth collide. In this way, God will be manifested through His people."

Bill Johnson, senior leader, Bethel Church, Redding, California; author, *God is Good* and *Hosting the Presence*

"Jesus came to set captives free, and through His triumph over death and hell, He has been ruled the Victor King. It is time for the Church to rise up and take its place. As a result of utilizing the truths found in this book, corrupt governments have been shifted and physical warring armies have been pushed back from the borders of nations. *God's Weapons of War* will give you the tools not only to fight but to win!"

Apostle Jane Hamon, senior pastor, Vision Church at Christian International

"Bishop Bill Hamon gives insight that is both meaty and a window into the future. This book will both challenge and encourage you to know what God is saying to the Church today."

Dr. Cindy Jacobs, president and co-founder, Generals International

"In *God's Weapons of War*, Dr. Bill Hamon shares revelation, prophetic insight and strategies that will inspire, inform and ignite a victorious passion within you and the emerging victorious Church. A must-read book for the victorious mindset necessary to advance the Kingdom of God in the last days!"

Dr. John P. Kelly, convenor, International Coalition of Apostolic Leaders

"While some in the prophetic movement have shunned spiritual warfare, the reality is God is activating an army—and the next great move will see this prophetic army of the Lord rise up with fervent faith. In *God's Weapons of War*, Bishop Bill Hamon expertly outlines what he practices—spiritual warfare that drives results. This is not your typical spiritual warfare book. It is filled with decades of victorious battle insights from a general of warfare. Every Christian needs to read this book."

Jennifer LeClaire, senior leader, Awakening House of Prayer; founder, Ignite Prophetic Network and Awakening Blaze prayer movement

"Bishop Hamon has been a great spiritual father to me whom I admire and respect very much. God used him to personally activate and mentor me in the prophetic many years ago. Therefore, I am in a unique position to testify not only about Bishop Hamon's powerful ministry, but also of his integrity, character and heart. He will always be an important voice of wisdom in my life that I honor and deeply respect."

Apostle Guillermo Maldonado, founder, King Jesus International Ministry

"Too often, in the war between the kingdoms of darkness and light, the Church loses by default. We must arm ourselves and engage the enemy in this war! I know of no one better equipped to teach on how to do so than Dr. Bill Hamon. No one!"

Dutch Sheets, president, Dutch Sheets Ministries

"Dr. Bill Hamon has written many books, but none is more important than *God's Weapons of War*. It is the most informative book on the purpose of the Church that I have ever read. God is raising up an army of worshiping warriors in these last days. Let's get ready for the greatest awakening the world has ever known!"

Ricky Skaggs, Spirit-filled, prophesying man of God; 2018 inductee, Country Music Hall of Fame

"Bishop Hamon's writings help keep me prophetically current with what God is doing in the Church today. *God's Weapons of War* is not just an informational prophetic proclamation. It is a book the Holy Spirit will use to align you for your highest participation in advancing the Kingdom of God. I am continually amazed at how Bishop Hamon catches the heart and timing of God. I make no apologies that I teach his material until it becomes my revelation also."

Dr. Sharon Stone, senior minister, Christian International Europe

"I am constantly amazed at Bishop Hamon's capacity for relevancy. *God's Weapons of War* brings all of his past teaching to a new convergence around the context of spiritual warfare. We need to talk about how believers can come together *as one* in the army of the Lord. This book should be issued to each soldier as a field guide for combat."

Dr. Lance Wallnau, director, Lance Learning Group

"We have entered a new era that will be marked by continuing conflict over the ultimate intention of God: the restoration of the kingdoms of this world back into His hands. Our actions to bring this about must reflect the seriousness of the conflict. Bishop Bill Hamon brilliantly deals with this issue and explains both the conflict and what our corresponding actions must be to win this war. I found this book extremely helpful and highly recommend it."

Barbara J. Yoder, lead apostle, Shekinah Regional Apostolic Center

"With powerful prophetic insight, Dr. Bill Hamon has given us the tools to help prepare the church for the harvest and battlefields ahead. Let us work together to strengthen the army of the Lord and advance God's Kingdom!"

Benny Hinn, pastor, Benny Hinn Ministries

GOD'S WEAPONS OF WAR

ARMING THE CHURCH TO DESTROY
THE KINGDOM OF DARKNESS

DR. BILL HAMON

Chosen

a division of Baker Publishing Group
Minneapolis, Minnesota

Published by Chosen Books
11400 Hampshire Avenue South
Bloomington, Minnesota 55438
www.chosenbooks.com

Chosen Books is a division of
Baker Publishing Group, Grand Rapids, Michigan

Printed in the United States of America

ISBN 978-0-8007-9914-4

Library of Congress Cataloging-in-Publication Data Control Number: 2018019478

Cover design by LOOK Design Studio

18 19 20 21 22 23 24   7 6 5 4 3 2 1

I dedicate this book to Jesus, my Commander in Chief, who made me a five-star general in His army of saints.

Jesus is waiting on His Church for all enemies to be made His footstool (see Hebrews 10:12–13), and I believe this book will motivate many saints to become active warriors and use their weapons of warfare to fulfill God's prophetic word. Jesus wants to return but cannot until all things are restored and all prophetic Scriptures are fulfilled (see Acts 3:21). God's World War III has been activated to subdue Christ's enemies and fulfill all prophecies. This must happen so that Jesus can be released from heaven to be joined with His Church forever.

We are co-laboring with You, Jesus, to train, equip and activate those called to be warriors in Your end time army.

Contents

Foreword

Christians must learn why it is imperative that we fight. We must begin to focus on the harvest battlefields ahead! Learning war comes easier to some than others; to those who grew up in relative peace and comfort, it may come hardest of all.

Why war? Why is it necessary? Why can people not live in harmony? These are the questions we ask our parents when we are first exposed to conflict through the media. We ask our history teachers when we are learning the events that brought us to the present. Most importantly, we ask God. "If you are a loving God," we question, "why do war and destruction occur?" The short answer is that we are called to serve in God's army of warriors. If we do not heed His call, the enemy will step in, and he will rule in our stead. We are called to possess, secure and protect our inheritance.

The times are a-changing—and we must understand the times. I know no other person still walking in the earth realm who better helps the Church understand the times than Bishop Bill Hamon. Dr. Hamon has created a masterpiece in *God's Weapons of War*. The Body of Christ, the saints of the ages, have corporately entered a season in which spiritual warfare is shifting to the harvest field that is called earth. The earth is the Lord's and the fullness thereof. This book reveals the corporate weapons of our warfare and divine decrees on how to use them as we engage in the battlefields of the future.

My own call from the Lord is to see the nations of the earth healed. One of my awesome privileges in doing this is to travel from nation to nation meeting with God's gathered people. Many nations still stand in the valley of decision. On January 1, 1984, I received a visitation of the Holy Spirit that changed my life and that of my wife, Pam. God revealed shifts in world events as He outlined strange happenings to come concerning the Soviet Bloc countries. After the Lord saw that He could trust me to pursue His purposes on a greater scale, He visited me on January 1, 1986, and revealed in detail changes that would come in ten-year cycles for the next forty years, ending in 2026.

God's army is being prepared for the battle ahead through these and other revelations that build the faith of His people. God does nothing on the earth without first revealing to His prophets what His will is in heaven (see Amos 3:6–7). This means He strips away secret plans of the enemy and opens up His overall plan, which eventually leads to the triumph of His people and the return of His Son to reign in the earth. His eyes run to and fro to see whom He may communicate with regarding His ultimate purposes of victory. I love Him, seek Him, walk with Him daily and am available for Him to communicate with. You can, too.

To help the Body shift into a mindset for war, I wrote *The Future War of the Church*, *God's Unfolding Battle Plan* and a number of other books. Much of what was written to prepare us is now a daily reality. One of the most misunderstood concepts in Christendom is the call of Christians to war. But God does not call us to war so that we can be defeated. I sense the season ahead to be the time of triumph; therefore, I recently wrote the companion to *God's Weapons of War*, a book titled

A Time to Triumph. I want to share some things in that book in order to shed light on how God is preparing the Body of Christ for the days ahead.*

A Vision of a New Movement

In September 2007, the Lord alerted me to a change in my life and its direction. He said, *Lay down your involvement in the prayer movement. I am going to reposition you and show you what is to come in days ahead. The prayer movement needs to be the wine for the wineskin that is forming. Look ahead to see a new wineskin.*

Through the next spring, I ministered as the Lord led me while I waited to find out where the Lord intended to reposition me. Then, on May 31, 2008, I joined John and Sheryl Price, Peter and Trisha Roselle, and other prophetic leaders in a time of intercession at Liberty State Park, across the Hudson River from Manhattan and in view of the Statue of Liberty. Millions of immigrants who arrived on the East Coast stopped first at Ellis Island to document their desire to be part of this nation. Many of them headed to the historic train station at Liberty State Park to catch a train that would take them to Newark or New York City. We gathered at this train station to "open the gates in 2008" for the glory of God to flood across America.

When worship began, the Spirit of God fell on me. I was caught up into a heavenly place, and I received a vision that stretched from the past into the future. In the vision, which lasted for four hours, I saw both demonic and divine strategies, historical and future paths, and small groups and nations. God, who is not in time, can open the eyes of the spirit man

* Sections of this foreword are adapted from Dr. Chuck D. Pierce, *A Time to Triumph: How to Win the War Ahead* (Minneapolis: Chosen, 2016), 12, 14, 146–152, 158–159, 166–167, 182. Used with permission.

to be able to see in a time that has not yet manifested—just as He did for Daniel, Jeremiah, the apostle John and many of the biblical prophets, who saw the time you and I are now living in and warned us of things to come. The Spirit of God lifts us into other realms so we can have hope and strategy for the future.

The first thing the Lord showed me was my own bloodline. I already knew the history of four generations on both sides of my family tree, and further back on my mother's side. The Lord showed me where the paths of my families intersected. He showed me where His Glory invaded our bloodline and also where demons had invaded and iniquitous structures had developed. I saw the progress Pam and I had made in overturning generational iniquities.

As worship continued, my spirit began to rise, as often happens during worship: We ascend high enough to have clear vision. Eventually, I could see the entire United States. The view was amazing, perplexing and confounding! I was caught between old and new paradigms and seasons of rule. First, He revealed His remnant, showing me where they were positioned. Next, He showed me their strength from state to state. He then invaded time and showed me the future, seven years ahead. Troops began to assemble from every place in each state, as though they were drawn by a powerful magnet, and gathered to form what looked like a river of glory fire.

"Who are these people, Lord?" I asked, and He said, *This is My triumphant reserve for the future!* I was peering into the future at what would become a new movement. His triumphant reserve would be called up for future Kingdom purposes. This was the new wineskin in a coming new movement. I saw this wineskin moving across America, and I asked, "Lord, how can America change?" He immediately responded, *My people must learn to play the trump card. If they do not, they will be ruled by a Jezebel spirit in the season ahead, as in the days of Athaliah.* (Remember that this was May 31, 2008, before Donald Trump had entered the political scene.)

The Triumphant People Arising

The movement of God's people—the river of glory fire—looked like liquid gold flowing in the land. It resembled fiery lava moving from state to state (every state had a movement). This group would destroy the works of the enemy in days ahead. Over the next seven years, by the Jewish New Year in September 2015, they would mature to be ready to go to war against the darkness attempting to bring destruction. Triumphant people are ones who know how to triumph, meaning to obtain victory, or a state of being victorious in conquest. Triumph carries a distinct emotion for God's children; in triumph, one expresses joy or exultation because he or she has prospered, succeeded and flourished.

An easy way to understand triumph is to think of a trump card, a card that takes all others ("trumping," or winning a hand or suit). The triumphant people I saw had the following characteristics:

- **They were infused with a victorious attitude.** Attitudes have a tremendous impact on how we see the world. Wrong attitudes can skew our perceptions and cloud our understanding of the fruits our labors are producing. Positioning your heart and mind on the Lord, however, will preserve you in times of trouble and lead to a victorious attitude. The Lord's triumphant people had strong hearts! Ask the Lord to adjust your attitude to triumph.

- **They were aligned for victory.** Alignment can be thought of as "snapping into place," the way a doctor must position a broken bone in its proper place in order for it to heal properly and the appendage to work again. An army must be aligned and ordered for victory. God has an order, and it will not manifest until we are properly aligned. The triumphant people were snapped into alignment for victory. To create the prototype of triumph for the future, we must be aligned in God's order: first apostles, second prophets, third teachers, then healers, miracle workers, administrators, etc. Review your present alignments.

- **They occupied a high-level aptitude to adjust quickly.** Adapting to the needs of battle and adjusting to overcome the strategies of the enemy require aptitude. A quick ability to apprehend something is not actually dependent on your intelligence but on your attitude. Those of lesser intelligence can have the highest aptitude, and those who should have high aptitude can be sabotaged by their shoddy attitudes or lack of commitment to being aligned. We have to have an attitude that enables us to adjust quickly against our enemy and toward God's order. That attitude and resulting alignment allows you to see as God sees, both the parts and how they fit together as a whole. Then, like a machine, all components are fit together exactly, allowing it to function.

- **They were creative, cunning (more shrewd than the enemy) and confrontational.** Creativity and cunning are like weapons the Lord has given us to elude and overpower our enemy. But to use them effectively, we have to be willing to *confront* the enemy, whether we want to or not. Consider how Jesus, led by the Spirit, confronted Satan in the wilderness: It was the bringing together of two opposing forces in which truth could be revealed through God's Word and prevail.

- In such confrontations, our creativity and cunning will give us the advantage. We will create the new from nothing. We will transform things into more prosperous forms or combine old forms into something with new qualities. And, though many Christians do not understand they are shrewder than the powers of darkness, we will outwit the enemy by our cunning, because our covenant relationship with God allows us to.

Learn to Play the Trump Card

We must learn to play the trump card, which God's Kingdom people hold in their hands. The world will be contended for by nations whose roots are still aligned with Babel. The earth is the Lord's, however, and the fullness thereof. The one determining force that is not listed among these nations is the triumphant reserve of the apostolic Church that is now rising. God has a Kingdom of people, a nation above all nations, who hold the "trump card" of influence over the world, the flesh and the devil. Built within God's children is His covenant authority to be used in a timely manner. When we exercise God's authority within us, we will overtake every plan of the enemy and release a strategy of fullness in the earth.

Attempting to plant doubt in Jesus' mind, Satan incited Him to dissatisfaction, impatience and self-will. Jesus' weapon in resisting this seduction was the Torah: He humbled Himself and quoted Deuteronomy 8:3, *"Man shall not live by bread alone; but man lives by every word that proceeds from the mouth of the LORD."* When Jesus used the Torah as a sword, the sword became life against the enemy and overcame his plan. This was the first trump card Jesus played.

Again the enemy played his own card, tempting Jesus based on His call. He will do the same to you. Since Jesus came to redeem the kingdoms of this world, the enemy offered the world to Jesus. But the offered gift came out of its proper time. Jesus used Deuteronomy 6:13 (AMP-CE) to counter him: *"You shall [reverently] fear the Lord your God and serve Him and swear by His name [and presence].*" Jesus did not compromise to gain dominion! As we learn to play the trump card of the Word at the right time, we triumph.

High Places and Ruling Demonic Centers Must Fall

When He lifted me up, the Lord showed me the high places erected by the enemy in the United States. These are the result of the worship war going on in each territory of the earth. As stated previously, worship occurs around the one whose throne has been established. We are made to worship; therefore, if we pay homage to the enemy, he will control the atmosphere. The entire territory then falls under the darkness of his presence. Demonic hosts redirect those in that territory away from God's plan of fullness, peace, joy and abundance.

I saw 23 states in America with covenant roots. Many states had freedom outposts, but He showed me where others were needed. Where the spiritual atmosphere was not yet conducive to freedom, He showed me how outposts could begin to form, changing the atmosphere and the land. Inside them I could hear sounds and see new types of warfare that will have to be developed by the triumphant people to regain new portions of the lands where they are located. I saw that prayer strategies from the last season will not be effective in the next. Nazareth and Capernaum are examples of this in Jesus' day. I thought of how the Lord told the disciples, "These will not come out except through prayer and fasting."

The truth is that for the believer in Christ, the best is always ahead. We have a wonderful promise for our future—the promise of eternal communion with God. The Bible clearly tells us that we should not live on earth with our sights set only on what is temporal; we should have a view of eternity and operate from heaven's perspective. God will give us grace to endure what is going on in our temporal world until we come into the fullness of our eternal destiny, which is with Him. This really is the bottom line. The war will intensify, but the best for God's children lies on the road ahead.

There is so much to understand in the coming war! This book, *God's Weapons of War*, will help you understand God as a warrior, the army of the Lord, the war ahead, the greatest corporate weapon for the Church in destroying the works of the devil, God's attitude toward war and, most importantly, your role in the season of triumph that we now live in. Discover new purposes in God's heart for creating mankind and what He wants from the human race.

Thank you, Bishop, for helping us become the triumphant reserve that God has planned to represent Him in the Kingdom war ahead!

Dr. Chuck D. Pierce, president, Global Spheres
and Glory of Zion International Ministries

1

The Army of the Lord Activated

One of the most important things for Christians in the 21st century to know is the times in which we live. We must know God's present-day purpose and what Christ Jesus is seeking to accomplish in and through His Church in this season, so that we can be co-laborers with Christ. There is a difference between working for Christ and working with Christ. Many ministers who represent past restoration movements are faithfully preaching the biblical truths that were restored in their movement and others. But we must not stop there, for God is still restoring and still doing new things in and through His Church. Some scriptural truths must be restored and divine purposes must be fulfilled before Jesus can return from heaven (see Acts 3:21; Hebrews 10:13). It is the Church's divine calling to bring about God's purposes on earth and usher in Jesus' return.

It is imperative that the 21st-century Church realize that the next emphasis of the Holy Spirit will be to activate the army of the Lord into *offensive warfare* and so fulfill God's present purpose for His Church. A few years ago, Cindy Jacobs prophesied to me, "Dr. Bill, Jesus is commissioning you to be a five-star general in the army of the Lord." Later someone gave me some documents explaining that five-star generals in America are only commissioned during a time of war. Now I lead churches in warfare as God's five-star general as often as I operate in my apostle-prophet calling as a fivefold minister. Prophets are motivated to warfare more than others because of what God said to the prophet Jeremiah in Jeremiah 1:10: "I have this day set you [the prophet] over the nations and over the kingdoms, to root out and to pull down, to destroy and to throw down [evil demonic principalities], to build and to plant" the Kingdom of God. (Throughout this book, I have used brackets for expansions/explanations of Scripture and italics for emphasis in Bible quotations.)

The purpose of *God's Weapons of War* is to enlighten and instruct Christian believers on how to do corporate spiritual warfare. Many books have been written about doing spiritual warfare as an individual for one's own deliverance, personal needs and victory over the enemy of our souls. Spiritual warfare has been taught as a good idea, and some have practiced spiritual warfare for themselves and others. But for those who want to co-labor with Christ in fulfilling His present-day purpose through His Church, knowing how to wage corporate spiritual warfare becomes an absolute necessity.

This is a ministry Christ has given me for His 21st-century Church; it is for me a passion and truth. In the mid-1990s, I had a vision in which Jesus introduced me to the archangel Michael. He introduced Michael by saying, *This is Michael, head general of My army of angels.* Then Jesus said, *Michael, this is Bill Hamon, one of My top generals in My army of saints.* When Jesus left us, we continued talking and strategizing on how we would win battles in our war with Satan and his evil spirit forces of darkness. On top of this, two mature prophets, at different times and places, prophesied that God had appointed me a five-star general in the army of saints.

And what is God preparing His army of saints for? First, some historical background: At certain points in the history of the Church, God has moved it into periods of restoration that have restored truths and ministries that had been lost. The period historians refer to as the Reformation was, in fact, the beginning of the Second Reformation of the Church, which for almost five hundred years (1517–2007) has restored the truths and ministries in the New Testament that were lost during the thousand-year dark age of the Church. The last movement within the Second Reformation was the saints movement activated in 2007. This led to the third and final Church Reformation, decreed from heaven in 2008. The purpose of this Third Reformation is to activate and fulfill all the truths and ministries that God has ordained for the last generation of the mortal church. The next Holy Spirit–directed move of God is the equipping and releasing of the army of the Lord to fight an offensive war, which in this book I am calling God's World War III.

God's Weapons of War covers God's purpose for declaring World War III against Satan and his spirit-world empire. It reveals the combatants in this war, the extent of the warfare, our weapons of warfare and how to use them, the final outcome and the rewards given to the overcomers who will fight to the end, winning this war by co-laboring with Christ Jesus, our mighty warrior.

God's World Wars

The Church has already entered God's World War III. For God to have a third world war, He must already have had a first and a second. God's World War I was fought to bring forth the Church, which was the First Reformation. In reality, it was the formation of the Church but a reformation for Israel, because it changed the entire way they related to God. In this Reformation, God made one new people from both Jew and Gentile to become the one Body of Christ, the Church.

At that time, God sent His Commander in Chief of the armies of heaven to earth as a human baby. He grew to a man, and at age thirty Jesus launched His campaign. His war was to destroy the works of the devil and provide redemption for mankind. Jesus fought—and won—His first major battle with the devil at His temptation in the wilderness, after which Father God anointed Jesus with the Holy Spirit and power. Jesus went about destroying the works of the devil by healing people of their devilish afflictions and casting out demons.

The winning battle took place on the cross, where Jesus provided redemption for mankind. Then, by His resurrection from the dead, He took the keys of death and hell from the devil. Jesus then birthed His Church and gave it power and authority over the devil and all his demons. Thereby the first world war was won.

God's World War II began in 1517 at the beginning of the Second Reformation. Its purpose was to restore the truth and all ministries lost during the dark age of the Church that lasted from AD 500 to 1500. The first shot in this war was fired in Germany on October 31, 1517, when God's general Martin Luther nailed his 95 Theses to the door of his church in Wittenberg. It required many battles fought through many restoration movements over 490 years to retake all the truths and ministries that the devil had captured during the dark age of the Church. Most of them had been restored back into the Church by the end of 2007, when the saints movement was birthed. Thereby God's second world war was won; the Second Reformation of the Church fulfilled God's divine purpose of restoring all New Testament truths and ministries that were alive and active in the first-century Church.

Now—in our generation—the Third Church Reformation has been birthed with the declaration of God's World War III in 2008.* God's chosen warriors and military officers were in intensified testing, training and equipping for seven years to prepare for the launching of God's offensive warfare in 2016.

We can find parallels between God's plan for His Church and Israel's history. For example, the movements through which God brought restoration to the Church during the Second Reformation are illustrated by Israel's experiences during their journey from Egypt to Canaan. The first of these movements, the Protestant movement of the early 1500s, brought the Church out of its Egyptian bondage (the dark age) of religious dead works. The sixth was the charismatic movement of the 1960s, which brought the Church to its Jordan River; in the seventh, the prophetic-apostolic movement of the 1980s, the Church crossed over the Jordan River into its Promised Land.

In the same way, Israel's seven-day march around Jericho typifies the seven years beginning in 2008. Israel's inheritance was the land of Canaan; the inheritance of the Church is the new earth. Israel was a few people, approximately two to three million, of which six hundred thousand were soldiers. Today, God's Kingdom people are in every nation of the world. God's charge to Joshua and the Israelite army was to make the kingdoms of Canaan the kingdom of Israel; this they accomplished by military conquest. The challenge to Christ's Church is to demonstrate the Kingdom of God in every nation until each nation becomes a goat or sheep nation. The sheep nations will come under the rule of the Kingdom of God (see Matthew 25:31–46). When Jesus returns to earth, all ungodly individuals and goat nations will be removed from earth and cast into the lake of fire. Then all nations remaining

---

* I have written a book covering the First, Second and Third Reformations titled *Prophetic Scriptures Yet to Be Fulfilled* (Destiny Image, 2010). It mostly discusses the Church demonstrating and establishing God's Kingdom.

on the earth shall come under the rule of Christ Jesus and His Kingdom saints.

Jesus has "made us kings and priests to our God; and we shall reign on the earth" (Revelation 5:10). We are destined to rule; Jesus declares in Revelation 2:26–27 that His Christian overcomers who keep fulfilling prophetic Scriptures until the end will rule and reign with Christ Jesus over the new earth. At that time the prophetic decree in Revelation 11:15 will be fulfilled, which declares that the kingdoms of this world have become the Kingdom of our God. When this is accomplished, God's World War III will be won; the third and final Church Reformation will have fulfilled its purpose. Those who have kept God's commandments and have overcome all things will reign with Christ over the nations with a rod of iron (see Revelation 2:26–27; 12:5; 19:15; 21:7).

Offensive Weapons for the Final Battle

This book will also reveal the final battle that will decisively win the war. We have entered an offensive war that will not end until Jesus personally leads His army of saints in the final battle. Now is the time that saints must know their weapons of war and how to use them. We absolutely have weapons of warfare that are mighty for the pulling down of Satan's strongholds (see 2 Corinthians 10:4; Ephesians 6:12). Pastors and all fivefold ministers must now function as drill sergeants and generals, diligently training the saints as soldiers who know how to fight as warriors in the army of our Commander in Chief.

We must make sure we are fully dressed in our protective defensive armor (Ephesians 6:10–18): our helmet of salvation, breastplate of righteousness, belt of truth and combat boots of the Gospel. The shield of faith, while mainly defensive, can also be used offensively. We must also be clothed with garments of salvation, garments of praise and the robe of righteousness (see Isaiah 61:3, 10).

We have an arsenal of offensive weapons as well: the sword of the Spirit, the name of Jesus, high praises, a shout of faith, tongues, prophetic acts and apostolic decrees. I have led numerous nations in warfare using the Church's greatest corporate weapon, the shout of faith, which explodes in the demonic spirit realm like an atomic bomb in the natural. Many ministers have testified of major changes and shifts in the nation after our acts of warfare and pulling down of strongholds. Our weapons of warfare are mighty in God for pulling down the strongholds of Satan (see 2 Corinthians 10:4).

The Next Great Move of God

This next great move will produce more manifestations of God's power and glory than ever recorded in Church history. It will continue until the glory of the Lord fills the earth as the waters cover the sea (see Numbers 14:21; Habakkuk 2:14). Jesus is calling forth tried and proven ministers to fulfill His present purpose and to co-labor with Him to win His World War III. At present we do not know for sure how many of the remaining prophetic Scriptures will be given to us to fulfill as Christ's mortal Church, in revelation and power. Fulfilling certain things will require that Christ return and immortalize His Church in order for them to become joint heirs and co-laborers with Christ in the fulfillment of all things. In the meantime, we are to do all that Christ gives us revelation, power and authority to accomplish for Him in fulfilling Christ's ultimate purpose for His mortal Church.

The world is now in a cyber war, the beginning of World War III in the natural, which will evolve into a military war of the nations. Meanwhile, the Church has entered its World War

III against spiritual beings, which will end with Jesus and His saints destroying antichrist, ungodly humans. Jesus told His Church to occupy until He comes (see Luke 19:13 KJV). To occupy has a military connotation that means more than holding territory—it means to keep fighting and possessing until . . . ! Ministers, let us now prepare Christian soldiers to be men and women of valor, mighty warriors like David's thirty mighty men, Gideon's three hundred and Joshua's conquering army. These special forces will fight alongside Jesus, the Commander in Chief of the angel army in heaven and the warrior saints on earth, until World War III is won. Be assured that Jesus with His victorious, overcoming warrior saints will win this war and triumph valiantly. They will then rule and reign over everything God has promised to His called, chosen and faithful overcomers (see Revelation 5:10; 17:14; Daniel 7:14, 18, 22, 27).

ENLIGHTENMENT, DECLARATION AND PRAYER

Father God, I believe we are living in the last days of the mortal Church. I pray that You will help me be knowledgeable of the times in which I live. I want to be a colaborer with You in fulfilling Your final purposes for Your Church and planet earth. By Your grace I will be conformed to Your likeness and give myself one hundred percent to Your service.

2

Mankind

A Special People for a Special Purpose

Before a proper understanding can be achieved concerning the Church and corporate spiritual warfare, we must first understand the reasons God created the human race. What does God want to accomplish in, through and with mankind? What potential power and creative capabilities did God give to man's mind and spirit? What power did He give him in his speech? Why would the eternal Creator create a being with so many of God's capabilities and then give him the power to have freedom of choice? If people only believe that God created man to have a relationship and fellowship with Him and to worship Him, then they will have a difficult time grasping God's many purposes for creating the human race. Let us examine the Scriptures and receive the mind of Christ to understand God's thinking and motivation for creating man on planet earth.

God's Original Purposes for Man

At some point in eternity past, God decided to create a new race of beings that would be unlike anything He had ever created. They would be unique, different from the cherubim, seraphim and angels that God had created endless ages before. God had reasons for doing this, and for His purposes to be fulfilled, this new creation had to be made a certain way and have certain attributes. They had to be more like their Creator than any creature God had ever created. In fact, this new creation, which God called man, would have to be created in God's own image and likeness. He had to be made comparable and compatible with God Himself in order for God to accomplish the many purposes He had in mind for man. God had a reason and purpose in every detail of His creation—in the forming of man's body, soul and spirit.

In my book *Who Am I and Why Am I Here* (Destiny Image, 2005), I discuss eight reasons God created the human race. Having a relationship with Him and worshiping Him are only two of those reasons. Another of God's original purposes for mankind was to reproduce through the power of procreation. God wanted to fill the earth with a race of beings in His own image and likeness. He could have created billions of human beings in one day and placed them all over the earth. But He did not do it that way. He only created one man and one woman and gave them the power to reproduce themselves.

Adam and Eve were to create all the rest of the men and women who were to fill the earth. They failed to fill the earth with a godlike race because of their disobedience to God's command not to eat of the evil tree, the Tree of Knowledge of Good and Evil. When the first man failed, God's purpose had to be postponed for four thousand years, until His Son came to earth and started a new creation in Christ, the race of mankind called the Church. Jesus sent the Holy Spirit and His fivefold ministers to work with the Church until it becomes a victorious Bride without spot or blemish, conformed to the image of Jesus Christ. Jesus and His Church fulfill seven of the eight purposes Father God had for creating the human race.

Why Earth and Not Heaven?

God did not choose to make man from some heavenly material, nor to form his body in heaven. God chose a planet called earth. He took earth material, dust, and formed man's body with it. God then breathed into man an eternal spirit. God knew man would not be able to fulfill His divine purpose by himself, so God created a special being that was comparable and compatible with the man. God presented her to Adam, and he called her woman and named her Eve. God planted a gigantic park with all kinds of trees, plants and flowers, producing every color and fragrance that would be pleasing to man. In this park were all kinds of vines growing vegetables, plus watermelons, cantaloupes and tropical trees bearing all kinds of citrus fruits and nuts. God named their great park the Garden of Eden. It had beauty and resources beyond imagination for supplying man with everything he would need to live in health and happiness.

As delightful as this place was, it was not heaven. In this, too, God had a purpose. It was necessary for God to create man from the earth and place man on the earth outside of the throne room of heaven. Because of God's many purposes and eternal plan for man, He knew that man would end up sinning and become subject to death. Man had to be created on a planet apart from heaven because sin and death could never be allowed in heaven.

Part of God's plan was for His Son to be born into the human family; God would be the Father and a young virgin woman would conceive and birth the Christ child. In this way it was possible for Jesus to become a mortal man who could suffer, bleed and die to provide redemption for mankind. This was God's special purpose, for it would give the opportunity for Him to demonstrate His core nature to all creation: God is love. All this was planned in the mind of God before He created the earth and mankind upon it. Jesus was "the Lamb slain from the foundation of the world" (Revelation 13:8), and Father God "chose us in [Christ] before the foundation of the world" (Ephesians 1:4).

Corruption of the Human Race

Though God had given His newly created man and woman every plant and tree for food, so that they could freely eat from anything that grew in the Garden, He added one exception. Of the two trees God planted in the middle of the Garden, Adam and Eve were allowed to eat only of the Tree of Life. They were commanded not to eat the fruit from the Tree of Knowledge of Good and Evil; if they ate from the evil tree, it would activate death within their bodies. The tree was placed there to test man's obedience to his Creator, for God had made mankind sovereign beings who could say no or yes to God or Satan, to good or evil—who could obey or disobey. They were created free moral agents with the power of choice. They had to be tested to determine their complete commitment to God and obedience to His commands.

Satan arrived, speaking through the serpent, and seduced Eve into eating of the evil fruit. She gave to Adam and he ate. This became the first sin committed by the human race. At this point God removed them from the Garden before they could eat of the Tree of Life after sinning. He sentenced them to death, which was and still is the penalty for disobedience. They were banished from the Garden and sentenced to hard labor outside in order to produce what they had freely enjoyed on the inside. Sin separated Adam and Eve from their inheritance in the Garden and their fellowship with God.

In addition, eating of the evil tree released evil in the world and gave the devil a legal right to begin his devilish work in the human race. This started with the murder of Abel by his brother Cain, bringing great heartbreak, grief and sorrow to Adam and Eve. Satan had tempted Eve with the promise that if she ate of the forbidden fruit, she would know and experience things she did not even know existed. She did! Adam and Eve experienced feelings of fear, shame, heartache, grief and all the sorrows and misery that sin can cause, eventually resulting in death to their bodies.

Why Give Man Freedom of Choice?

God could have saved Adam and Eve and even Himself from all that we just described if He had created man like a computer. He could have designed him to be a humanoid robot, doing only what God programmed within him—God could just push a button that would make man worship, work or anything God wanted man to do. But God did not want a machine. He did not even want an employee or slave. He wanted sons and daughters, fellow beings with His nature and likeness. Ones who freely chose to love, obey and relate to God as a comparable and compatible fellow being. He did not want them to stay babes, innocent and immature their lives long, but to grow in grace and knowledge until they could communicate and cooperate with God in fulfilling all the purposes for which the Eternal One created the mortal human race.

God's original plan and desire was for man and God to live and work together, thereby enabling God to fulfill His eternal purposes through humans (see Ephesians 1:11; 3:11). God's intent and desire was not for man and God to be separated from each other. God wanted man to be His friend and trustworthy co-laborer with the heart and mind of God. Father God wanted mankind to have heaven on earth—for God's will to be done on earth with mankind as His will and way were done with His angels in heaven. That is one reason Jesus taught us to pray, "Thy Kingdom come, Thy will be done on earth as it is in heaven."

I am presenting this in such detail to reveal the type of man creature that God wanted and needed in order to fulfill His purpose in creating the human race. When man becomes so sinful as to grow depraved and corrupt—the opposite of everything God intended and wanted man to be—he becomes worthless. He has no value for God, for God cannot relate to or use such a one to fulfill His purposes. Because of this, mankind is not even fit to be on the beautiful earth prepared for them. God's only alternative, in order to fulfill His purpose in and through mankind, is to remove the wicked from the earth.

Transitioning to Hell or New Earth?

This He did about 1600 years after Adam and Eve were cast out of Paradise Park (the Garden of Eden). By this time mankind had degenerated into extreme evil, wickedness and ungodliness (which is un-God-likeness). God found one man by the name of Noah who was righteous in that ungodly generation. The Eternal told Noah to build an ark for himself, his wife, their three sons and their wives, and to bring with them a sample of all land and air creatures into the Ark. They were to be the remnant that would make it to the new world to preserve and continue the human race and the created beings who occupied the land and air. God planned to send a flood of water that would so cover the world that it would rise twenty feet above the highest mountain peak. He would do this by releasing torrential rains for forty days and nights and by opening the fountains of the earth for underground water to burst forth. Every living, breathing thing on earth would be destroyed.

Why would God do this? Because the people He had created with freedom of choice had become more aligned with Satan and his demonic spirit beings than they were with God and His holy angels. God decided to remove them all from His earth and send them to Satan's domain, hell. Hell was originally created for Lucifer and his fallen angels, but God decreed that all humans who rebelled against His way of life and His authority over them would be sentenced to Satan's eternal destiny:

> When the Lord God saw the extent of human wickedness, and that the trend and direction of men's lives were only towards evil, he was sorry he had made them. It broke his heart. And he said, "I will blot out from the face of the earth all mankind that I created. Yes, and the animals too, and the reptiles and the birds. For I am sorry I made them."
>
> . . . Meanwhile, the crime rate was rising rapidly across the earth, and, as seen by God, the world was rotten to the core. As God observed how bad it was, and saw that all mankind was vicious and depraved, he said to Noah, "I have decided to destroy all mankind; for the earth is filled with crime because of man. Yes, I will destroy mankind from the earth."
>
> Genesis 6:5–7, 11–13 TLB

When preaching about God as a mighty warrior, I often make the rather shocking statement that I can show you in the Old Testament where God killed more people than He saved. This is a good example. Historians have determined that there were approximately 20 million people living on planet earth when God sent the Flood; if this is true, then He killed 19,999,992 and saved 8. At the same time, God saved righteous Noah and his family in the Ark in order to preserve and continue the human race on earth. God could not simply take them to heaven, as we shall see, for he needed mortal man on planet earth to fulfill His number one purpose for creating man: to take on a mortal human body in order to die on the cross and reveal God's core nature of love.

Hating Evil Is God's Nature

It is important to understand that God's willingness to destroy corrupted mankind flows from His love and goodness. When one apple becomes rotten in a bowl of apples, you have to throw that apple in the garbage, or it will contaminate the rest. God hates all that perverts and makes man opposite of everything that God planned for man to be and do. Evil is likened to darkness; God is light and there is no darkness in Him. Light and darkness cannot dwell together. God's truth exposes and destroys error.

To hate means something is detestable to you. It is the opposite of everything you like and enjoy—opposite of everything you think is right, beautiful and upstanding. If you hate evil, you have no affinity with it; your whole soul is repulsed at the very thought and sight of evil and un-God-likeness. Hating evil is an attribute of God just as loving people is. God anointed Jesus above his fellows because He "loved righteousness and hated iniquity" (Hebrews 1:9 KJV). If we truly love righteousness, then we should also hate iniquity.

Some have claimed that the God of the Old Testament was the one who hated, while Jesus never hated anyone or anything. He was just pure, sweet love. But Jesus also hated, for He said, "You hate the deeds of the Nicolaitans, which I also *hate*" (Revelation 2:6; see also verse 15). According to the Bible, there are many things God hates; in Proverbs 6:16–19 He lists six, and a seventh that was an abomination to Him:

1. **A proud look:** full of pride, haughty, egotistical, self-importance
2. **A lying tongue:** deceitful, dishonest, exaggeration, betrayal
3. **Hands that shed innocent blood:** talebearer, gossiper, jealousy, murder, abortion
4. **Heart that devises wicked plans:** vengeful, bad motives, lust
5. **Feet that are swift in running to evil:** quick-tempered, unstable
6. **A false witness who speaks lies:** false accuser, untrustworthy
7. **One who sows discord among brethren**

God not only hates the seventh on the list but despises it with a passion. It makes Him very angry, because it is an abomination for someone to cause division and sow discord among His special people whom Jesus redeemed to be one united Body of Christ. This brings God's judgment on the Christian who does it.

In Isaiah 1:10–20 God declares that His soul hates hypocrisy in all forms, especially when His people perform religious activity with sin and rebellion in their lives:

> Incense is an abomination to Me. The New Moons, the Sabbaths, and the calling of assemblies—I cannot endure iniquity and the sacred meeting. Your New Moons and your appointed feasts *My soul hates*; they are a trouble to Me, I am weary of bearing them. When you spread out your hands, I will hide My eyes from you; even though you make many prayers, I will not hear.
>
> Verses 13–15

In Proverbs 8:13, the wisdom of God declares that, "The fear of the LORD is to *hate* evil; pride and arrogance and the evil way and the perverse mouth I *hate*." "You who *love* the LORD, *hate* evil!" (Psalm 97:10).

God loves people so much that He gave His only begotten Son to die on the cross and shed His life's blood for the redemption of man. But if people refuse God's redemption and continue in their wicked ways, then God has no alternative but to judge them and separate them forever from the righteous by denying their entrance into heaven. People who practice ungodliness and the prideful selfishness of Lucifer can never be allowed to enter heaven, regardless of who they are. For God to allow evil, rebellion, self-will against God's will and all that is contrary to the character of Christ Jesus to enter into and remain in His heavenly Kingdom would negate God's purpose for creating mankind. God removed Lucifer from heaven's domain because of his self-will, self-promotion and rebellion against God's sovereign authority. It is certain that the Holy One will not allow a human into heaven with the same spirit and attitude as Lucifer!

Why Did God Continue the Human Race?

Out of the entire human population God was only able to find one man who was living according to God's way of life. God chose and commissioned Noah and his family to preserve and transition the human race to a new earth. One might ask why God did not rapture Noah and his family to heaven and blow up planet earth with all the wicked people. Since the first prototype of man was found to be faulty and did not perform according to God's standard, why did God not find another planet, make a new man and start all over? Maybe He could design a new man who would not disobey God or fail to fulfill the Creator's purpose for a mankind creation living outside of heaven.

There are several reasons why He did not. One major reason God continued the human race with Noah was because of

God's number one purpose for creating man: in order to suffer, bleed and die on the cross for mankind, thereby revealing to all creation that God is love. God knew when He made man a free moral agent that he would eventually sin. That is the reason Jesus Christ was slain on the cross, in the mind and purpose of God, from the foundation of the world (see Revelation 13:8). The Bible also says we were chosen in Christ before the foundation of the world (see Ephesians 1:4).

As long as man was in the Garden, sinless and eating of the Tree of Life, he could have lived indefinitely. When Adam and Eve followed Satan's deceitful suggestions and ate the forbidden fruit, however, instead of following God's command not to eat of the evil tree, God had to remove them from the Garden. For God to fulfill one of His major purposes for creating the human race, man had to be separated from the Tree of Life; God could not allow them to eat of it in a sinful state. Therefore, He drove them out and shut the entrance, hiding the Garden so that no future generation of mankind could find it. This caused the human body to become mortal, subjecting it to suffering, bleeding and dying. For God planned for His Son to come to earth and take on a mortal human body. Jesus needed that type of body so that he could go to the cross and suffer, bleed and die for the redemption of mankind.

Man's Perspective versus God's Purpose

Some wonder, "Why would God create a race of beings that would result in His Son having to come and suffer and die to provide redemption for His creation?" From man's perspective, Calvary came about because of man's sinful state. From God's personal purpose, the human race was created to produce Calvary. God planned the whole thing concerning the human race *in order* to bring about Calvary. God wanted an opportunity to demonstrate to all of His creation what motivated Him to do all that He did—create the cherubim, seraphim, angels and especially His masterpiece, mankind. No one knew the core being of God. They knew He was all-powerful, all-knowing and everywhere present, that He was the Creator of all things; but that did not reveal to them what motivated God to do these things. Was He an egotistical being who did it for His own pleasure? Were His creations merely playthings for Him?

God had no way of revealing that His core being, His nature and His motivation were love (*agape*). The kind of love that God is cannot be demonstrated just by giving things or creating heaven, earth and the universe. God's love can only be demonstrated by the sacrificial giving of oneself. He needed a means by which He could give Himself sacrificially for His creation.

Some have wondered, "Why didn't God demonstrate His love by dying for Lucifer and his fallen angels instead of creating a whole new race of beings?" There are two major reasons: One is that God is the Eternal, and no part of Him could ever die. The other is that angels are one single entity—spirit beings. One sin and they were lost forever. Thank God that you are not an angel.

God had to have a creation that would be an eternal spirit being clothed in a mortal body that could suffer, bleed and die. When death took place, the eternal spirit of man would separate from the body and continue to exist. When God created man, He created for him a body out of the dust of the earth and then breathed an eternal spirit into him. Man became a natural, physical entity with an inner spirit being. God gave Adam and Eve the procreative power to reproduce other human beings. He did this for three major reasons: First, God only intended to create one man and one woman; they would have to bring about the rest of the human race through generations of reproduction. Second, God planned in the fullness of time to come to earth and impregnate a young virgin woman in order to produce a human body that He could live in as a human being. This human being would be called the Son of God and named Jesus. This fulfilled God the Father's eternal desire to beget a biological Son. Adam was a created son, but Jesus was a biological Son. Third, God would demonstrate through this mortal body His core being of love. He would reveal His concern for mankind by healing them and delivering them from the works of the devil. But to demonstrate His *agape* love, He would give that body to be crucified on the cross and shed His life's blood to reconcile man back to Himself. Then all eternal beings in heaven and earth would be able to know that *God is love*.

> God demonstrates His own love toward us, in that while we were still sinners, Christ died for us.
>
> Romans 5:8

> We have known and believed the love that God has for us. *God is love*, and he who abides in love abides in God, and God in him.
>
> 1 John 4:16

> For this is the love of God, that we keep His commandments.
>
> 1 John 5:3

> He who does not love does not know God, for God is love. In this the love of God was manifested toward us, that God has sent His only begotten Son into the world, that we might live through Him. In this is love, not that we loved God, but that He loved us and sent His Son to be the propitiation for our sins. Beloved, if God so loved us, we also ought to love one another.
>
> 1 John 4:8–11

> By this we know love, because [Jesus] laid down His life for us.
>
> 1 John 3:16

God so loved the world that He gave His only begotten Son,
that whoever believes in [Jesus] should not perish but have everlasting life.

John 3:16

God's Relationship with Mankind

One reason God created man in His image and likeness was
because He planned to become a man among the human race.
When Father God was creating Adam's body, He had in mind
the type of body He wanted His Son to have. He would accomplish this by sending His Son to earth to be born of a human
woman. A baby takes its DNA and physical characteristics from
its parents; therefore, Jesus received His divine DNA from His
Father. God would live on earth in the body of Jesus as one of
the human race for approximately 34 years, from conception
to crucifixion. The fullness of the Godhead lived in the body
of Jesus: "For in Him dwells all the fullness of the Godhead
bodily" (Colossians 2:9)—or, as it is translated in The Living
Bible, "For in Christ there is all of God in a human body."

The human race was to be God's kind of people, a godly
race. His original man, Adam, failed to maintain what God had
established for him. But that did not hinder God's overall plan,
for He had a Second Man in mind—the man Christ Jesus, who
would be Father God's perfect man and mankind's perfect God.
The man Christ Jesus would give His life's blood on the cross to
reconcile mankind back to God. Those who would accept the
blood of Jesus for cleansing from their sins would be born into
the family of God. They would be known as children of God
and members of Christ's Church. They would become joint
heirs with Christ Jesus as they were conformed to His image.
These new creations of mankind are called and destined to
fulfill the Eternal's overall purpose for creating the human race.

God and the Human Race

All true Christians agree that God created the human race. It was eternal God's idea and desire to bring into being living people. God carefully fashioned man just the way He wanted in body, soul and spirit. Jehovah God knew the eternal plan and purpose He had for the human race. He knew man would eventually eat of the Tree of Knowledge of Good and Evil. But God had yet a greater plan for man by sending His Son to be the Tree of Life for mankind. Jesus would birth the Church and put its people in a new garden, described as "the heavenly places in Christ Jesus" (Ephesians 2:6; see also Ephesians 1:20). This was a place like the Garden, which provided every need of mankind. That place gives man power and authority over the spirit world of Satan, just as Adam was given authority over the natural world: "Behold, I give you the authority to trample on serpents [the devil] and scorpions [demons], and over all the power of the enemy" (Luke 10:19).

God knew that man would sin and become mortal, but this was necessary for God to fulfill some of His purposes for creating mankind. The Eternal also knows when Jesus will come back to earth to resurrect and translate His Church into the immortal human Church race. God is the Alpha and Omega, the beginning and the end. He knows how and when He will remove the wicked from the earth, purifying it with His cleansing fire and making a new earth, where only righteousness exists and rules (2 Peter 3:13). God knows the eternal purpose He has for His immortalized Church to fulfill throughout the endless ages of eternity (see Ephesians 3:11, 21).

In other words, when God made man, He had in mind every purpose man was to fulfill in His mortal state and the eternal relationship and work His Church would have with Him throughout eternity. Every part of man's body, soul and spirit was designed with God's overall eternal purpose for man in mind. Everything God does has a purpose and design to help Him fulfill His greater plan for man on earth and in heaven above. If you have been chosen and redeemed by God the Father through our Lord Jesus Christ, then you should be so thankful that you are willing to give your all.

ENLIGHTENMENT, DECLARATION AND PRAYER

Lord Jesus, You gave Your life's blood on the cross to redeem me for Yourself. Such love is beyond my human comprehension. Because of Your great love for me, the great price You paid for my redemption and the amazing eternal plan You have for my life, I give myself completely to You to do whatever necessary to conform me to Your image and likeness, while fulfilling Your every purpose for my life. Amen.

3

A God Who Makes War

In chapter 2, I shared God's purpose in creating mankind to be a people through whom He could beget His own Son, Jesus. I wanted to start with that foundational truth in order to reveal why God makes war with mankind, which will happen in His World War III. God makes war in order to fight for His people. When Jesus returns to earth as King of kings and Lord of lords, according to the Bible, "in righteousness He judges and makes war" with the wicked antichrist humans on the earth (Revelation 19:11–21).

When I teach about God being a warrior and killing large numbers of people, the way He did when He sent the Flood in the days of Noah, people have questions: If God loved the world enough to give His Son, and if His desire is that all mankind should be saved and come to the knowledge of the truth . . . how could He at the same time be willing to end a person's life, knowing that person would go to hell?

A thorough answer to that question would require a book (though I give many answers in this book). Remember, God is one God, but He has many attributes, convictions, criteria and divine principles and practices concerning all of creation. He is both a roaring lion and a meek lamb. He comes riding a white charger, a sharp sword in His mouth, and He stands outside the door of His Church, knocking and asking if He may be let in. That is the reason the apostle Paul declares in Romans 11:22 that we must understand both the goodness and severity of God.

This is revealed in God's dealings with His great and glorious worship leader, Lucifer. When Lucifer conceived the idea of self-will and rebellion, even taking over God's throne, God directed General Michael and his warrior angels to cast Lucifer out of heaven, along with one third of the angels, whom he had convinced to follow him. This marked the beginning of sin, rebellion and hell. But it was the love and mercy of God that drove Him to cast Lucifer out of His Kingdom; if He had not, Lucifer could have corrupted all of God's heavenly universe. If he had gained God's throne, he would have forced all God's creation to be wicked and evil, just as he had become.

Remember that God made man a free moral agent, comparable to and compatible with God Himself. Man has freedom to make his own choices apart from God or the devil. Man was made in God's own image and likeness, a special race that God made to be His people. When mankind chooses to become more like the devil than God, then God must remove them forever out of his Kingdom and send them to Satan's, which is hell.

The Bible declares in 1 Corinthians 2:14 that man by his natural reasoning cannot comprehend the ways of God. To the natural mind, the concept of condemning humans to eternal hell is so inhumane as to seem ungodlike. That is why false doctrines on this subject abound, such as the doctrine of universalism, invented in the 1600s by a preacher who taught that at the end of time all humans will enter God's Kingdom, and the devil and all of his fallen angels will be restored back to God and heaven. Or the false doctrine of inclusion, invented in the twentieth century by a Pentecostal preacher, which teaches that all men were saved automatically when Jesus died on the cross, though many do not know it yet. (They will appreciate it, the reasoning goes, when they get to heaven.)

Human reasoning will always lead human beings to false doctrines like these. A person cannot understand God's eternal purposes and the reasons for what He does by human reasoning and emotional sentimentality. Be assured that God almighty as revealed through Jesus Christ is just and righteous, and He does all things from His wisdom and love.

God committed Himself to the human race when He created man. Even though God's original man failed, that did not and will not stop God from working with mankind until He accomplishes all of His purposes for creating man. God is intricately involved in the human race, and He will continue the mortal race of mankind until every purpose for which He created mankind is fulfilled. Most of them have been fulfilled, but some are still in the final stages of fulfillment.[*]

A Worthy Opponent

In order to accomplish His purposes, God chose Abraham to be the father of a special race within the human race that would be known as God's people, and He chose Israel as His special nation. In the New Testament, Christ's Church is God's special spiritual people, and Israel is still recognized as God's natural people and nation. God counts His redeemed people worthy to be the Bride of Christ. In this book I will show how God continually got involved in saving both His spiritual and natural people by destroying human enemies.

When Lucifer rebelled against God, the Almighty did not get off His throne to fight with him. He sent Michael, His general

---

[*] As I mentioned in the first chapter, the eight major purposes God created man for are described in detail in my book *Who Am I and Why Am I Here* (Destiny Image, 2010). In chapter 1 of my book *How Can These Things Be?* (Destiny Image, 2014), I give the stage of fulfillment for each of these eight purposes.

over the armies of heaven, and had him fight Lucifer and his angels. Michael and his warring angels defeated Lucifer and his fallen angels, casting them out of heaven and throwing them back on earth.

This is not what will happen at the end of the age, however. When the time comes for wicked mankind to be subdued, destroyed and cast off the earth, Jesus Himself will lead the saintly and angelic warriors to fight against mankind. Fallen angels were not worthy opponents for God; their opposition did not stir Him to personally get involved in the fight. But when it comes to the human race, God counts wicked people as worthy opponents to fight and, yes, sometimes kill.

God told Pharaoh, "For this very purpose I have raised you up, that I may show My power in you, and that My name may be declared in all the earth" (Romans 9:17). Jesus came to earth not only to provide redemption for mankind but also "that He might destroy the works of the devil" (1 John 3:8). Jesus declared that he was commissioning His followers just as Father God commissioned Him when He prayed, "[Father,] as You sent Me into the world, I have also sent them into the world" (John 17:18). He was sending them forth with the same authority to destroy the works of the devil that His Father had given Him. If they would fully believe in Him, they would be able to do everything that Jesus did and more: "He who believes in Me, the works that I do he will do also; and greater works than these he will do" (John 14:12). May God grant the spirit of wisdom and revelation to be ours so that we may know the full power that is available to us (see Ephesians 1:18–20).

Finished Work and a Time of Waiting

Jesus cried out on the cross, "*It is finished!*" In His prophetic prayer in John 17:4, He declared, "I have finished the work which You have given Me to do" in the flesh. After Jesus arose from the grave and birthed the Church, He gave all of His power and ministry to the Church, which is His corporate Body, the Body of Christ. Every member of Christ's corporate Body has a membership ministry. Jesus divided His ministry to the Church into five different parts (known as gifts or ministries) and distributed them among certain members of His Church. He called these five ministries apostles, prophets, evangelists, pastors and teachers. These are headship ministries representing Christ Himself to His Church. They are given to fulfill Christ's decree, "I will build My Church." They are equippers of the saints and builders of Christ's Church.

God the Father was in Christ reconciling the world unto Himself. He fulfilled many of His purposes for creating the human race in and through the mortal body of Jesus. After Jesus had finished all the work Father God had planned to accomplish through Him, He ascended to heaven and sat down at the right hand of the Father. The Father agreed that Jesus had accomplished everything in the flesh for which He was predestined. He also fulfilled all the Jewish Messianic prophecies (see Acts 3:18). Now Father God told His Son to "sit at My right hand, till I make Your enemies Your footstool" (Hebrews 1:13).

Jesus has been "from that time *waiting* till His enemies are made His footstool" (Hebrews 10:13). He is anxious to personally come again and lead His Church in their war against their enemies. But Jesus knows that He has turned everything over to His corporate Body to fulfill all that must be fulfilled before His second coming can happen. Until then Jesus is received in heaven and is retained there by the Father "until the times of restoration of all things, which God has spoken by the mouth of all His holy prophets since the world began" (Acts 3:21).

By His Spirit, Christ will fulfill in His Church everything the Body of Christ is supposed to restore and fulfill—up until Christ's second coming in His resurrected and glorified human body (see Acts 1:11). At that time Jesus will restore to His departed saints their earthly bodies by His resurrection power. At the same time, He will transform the bodies of the living saints into immortal bodies. They will all be joined together as they meet the Lord Jesus in the air (see 1 Thessalonians 4:13–18). Jesus will lead His overcomer warriors in the final battle against all ungodly humanity on earth. The major deceivers of the world, such as the beast, false prophets and all antichrists, will be cast alive into the lake of fire (see Revelation 19:11–21).

At the same time a mighty angel from heaven, probably Michael, will bind Satan and cast him into the bottomless pit. Jesus and His Church will establish the rule of the Kingdom of God over all the earth for a thousand years. Then,

> when the thousand years have expired, Satan will be released from his prison and will go out to deceive the nations which are in the four corners of the earth, Gog and Magog, to gather them together to battle, whose number is as the sand of the sea. They went up on the breadth of the earth and surrounded the camp of the saints and the beloved city. And fire came down from God out of heaven and devoured them. The devil, who deceived them, was cast into the lake of fire and brimstone where the beast and the false prophet are. And they will be tormented day and night forever and ever.
>
> Revelation 20:7–10

Enoch, the seventh from Adam, prophesied more than five thousand years ago about this end time battle that Jesus and His warrior saints will fight and win: "Behold, the Lord comes with ten thousands of His saints, to execute judgment on all, to convict all who are ungodly among them of all of their ungodly deeds which they have committed in an ungodly way, and of all the harsh things which ungodly sinners have spoken against [Jesus Christ]" (Jude 14–15). "To execute on them the written judgment—this honor have all His saints" (Psalm 149:9). The Lord of Hosts says of His saintly warriors, "You are My battle-ax and weapons of war: for with you I will break the nation in pieces; with you I will destroy kingdoms" (Jeremiah 51:20).

Main Purposes of the Third Reformation

As we come closer to that time, God is beginning this Third Church Reformation to prepare and commission His soldiers to fight the spiritual World War III. The following eleven points give us a glimpse into God's purposes for the Third Reformation:

1. To fulfill all prophetic Scripture not yet fulfilled.
2. To transform the restored Church into a victorious, over-coming warrior Church.
3. To demonstrate the Kingdom of God with supernatural power as a witness to every nation that Jesus is the only true Savior and God for mankind.
4. To disciple the nations until each becomes a sheep or goat nation.
5. To restore all and fulfill all things that must be fulfilled so the second coming of Jesus can take place.
6. To equip and activate God's saint army to subdue Christ's enemies until they are made His footstool.
7. To equip and commission the seven-mountain saints to be kingdom influencers in their spheres of influence. Many are to be positioned like Joseph in Egypt, Daniel in Babylon, Esther in Persia and Deborah in Israel.
8. To release the army of the Lord to prepare the way for the Kingdom-establishing movement, which will bring about the final preparation for the Second Coming of Christ in

which He will be accompanied by His armies in heaven and earth to remove the wicked from the earth. When God's appointed angel casts Satan into the bottomless pit for a thousand years, then Jesus will set up His rule and Kingdom over all the earth with His joint heir, the Church. This will be heaven on earth for a thousand years.

9. To reap the greatest harvest of souls ever recorded in Church history.

10. To allow the fivefold ministers to complete their commission of building and perfecting the Body of Christ until it is matured into Christ's likeness, manifesting the miraculous ministry of Christ Jesus.

11. To allow the knowledge of the glory of God to continue increasing until the glory of the Lord fills the earth as the waters cover the sea.

The warriors of God's World War III will spearhead most of these purposes. They will be like Gideon's three hundred, like Jonathan and his armor bearer attacking the Philistine fort containing hundreds of warriors, and like David standing against the giant Goliath. They will have the spirit of Joshua and Caleb, who led the Israelite army in conquering and possessing Canaan.

The challenge is that we do not absolutely know for sure how much Christ's Church will do while in their mortal bodies and how much they will fulfill as His immortal Church. We do know that we are to occupy until He comes. We must seek to accomplish everything He has shown us that yet needs to be fulfilled. When Jesus sees that His overcoming warrior Church has done all that can be done in its mortality, then He will shout as He descends from heaven to immortalize His Church. They can then join Him as the immortal saint army to finish fulfilling all of God's purposes for creating the human race.

Do Your Best, God Will Do the Rest

When we have done our best, God will do the rest. Jonathan and his armor bearer are a good example of this principle. In 1 Samuel 14:1–23, a restless Jonathan decided he did not want to wait out a stalemate between the Israelite and Philistine armies. The Philistines were ruling over Israel at that time, and they had established forts throughout Israel. After Jonathan and his thousand soldiers attacked one of the forts holding several hundred Philistine soldiers, the Philistines were infuriated. They gathered their whole army, three thousand chariots (or, according to some biblical manuscripts, as many as thirty thousand!), six thousand horsemen and foot soldiers so numerous they could not be counted. Several thousand Israelites gathered with King Saul at the sound of his alarm, but when his soldiers heard how vast the coming army was, they began to abandon the Israelite army and hide wherever they could. Only about six hundred remained with Saul.

Jonathan decided to take a step of faith. He alone, with his armor bearer, quietly slipped away from their camp to expose themselves to a garrison of the enemy. Jonathan clarified the sign they would receive as confirmation from God that they were to engage the Philistines in battle: If the Philistines told them to come up to the garrison, they would go up to fight.

Indeed, they called to Jonathan and his armor bearer to come, and the two climbed up the steep hill on their hands and knees. Let me tell you how I imagine this scene playing out: When they stepped in the courtyard of that garrison, hundreds of Philistine warriors ready to meet them, one big, mean, ugly warrior told the rest of them to stand back so he could finish the two lads in short time. Jonathan, armed with a sword (his helper only had a war club), ducked nimbly from the swing of his enemy's huge sword. He quickly sliced with his own sword and almost cut the man's leg off; then Jonathan rammed his sword into the warrior's side. The soldier fell, and Jonathan's armor bearer crushed his head with his club. Meanwhile Jonathan engaged in a sword fight with the next soldier. He wounded him and brought him to the ground, while his helper dashed his brains with his club, killing him.

The Bible declares this continued for a while until they had killed twenty Philistine soldiers. Hundreds of Philistine warriors were present. There was no way that Jonathan would have been able to kill all five hundred men. God saw that he had done his best, so God stepped in and did the rest. He activated an earthquake—perhaps he even sent thunder and lightning bolts into their midst. At the same time Michael and his war angels swept into that fort and put terror and confusion in the Philistines. In panic they blindly swung their swords in every direction, in so doing killing one another. The Israelites who had been drafted into the Philistine army started killing Philistines, too, and the Israelite soldiers who had hidden themselves came out and joined in chasing and killing the Philistines.

Think about it! One young man dared to believe God could work miracles for him on behalf of his nation. He exposed himself to the enemy and engaged in warfare that set a nation free from its oppressors and established Israel as a nation of its own. Jonathan is a living example of the type of warriors who will fight in God's World War III.

The same principle worked for Gideon and his three hundred warriors when they attacked the Midianite camp in Judges 7. Again their enemies were too numerous to count. Gideon and his tiny band of warriors made all the necessary preparations; then they blew their trumpets and let their torches burn brightly while shouting, "The sword of the Lord and of Gideon!" At midnight they woke up hundreds of thousands of warriors. They did their part, and then God did His. He sent General Michael and his war angels to sweep down into the Midianite camp, imparting to them a spirit of terror and confusion. In frenzied fear they started swinging their swords at anything that moved, thus killing each other, and running for their lives. When we do our best, then God will supernaturally do the rest. We do not have to try to figure out how it is possible to accomplish that much when we are going against impossible odds, with no possibility of winning. God is looking for those who will step out and attempt to do the impossible so that He can supernaturally give them the victory.

ENLIGHTENMENT, DECLARATION AND PRAYER

Heavenly Father, You created the universe, our solar system and planet earth. You chose earth to create man's body from its dust. You formed a being in Your image and likeness. Your Word reveals that You cannot relate to mankind unless they have been made a new creation in Christ Jesus and are continually being conformed to His likeness. Father God, help me be like Jesus so that I can have fellowship with You as a true child of God. I stand on the truth revealed in this chapter, that when I have done my best, then God will do the rest. I know as I commit myself to You that You will fight for me to destroy my enemies.

4

Knowing God's Time of Visitation

By the time Jesus was born, the Jews had been praying, fasting and crying out for centuries for the Messiah to come. And yet when He began ministering publicly, they missed Him.

> Now as [Jesus] drew near, He saw the city [of Jerusalem] and wept over it, saying, "If you had known, even you, especially in this your day, the things that make for your peace! But now they are hidden from your eyes. For days will come upon you when your enemies will build an embankment around you, surround you and close you in on every side, and level you, and your children within you, to the ground; and they will not leave in [your Temple] one stone upon another, *because you did not know the time of your visitation.*"
>
> Luke 19:41–44

Instead of recognizing Jesus as their long-awaited Messiah, the Jewish priests and leaders rejected Him and crucified Him, and thereby they missed their appointed time of divine visitation from heaven. Because the Jews refused their day of visitation,

Jesus prophesied the destruction of Jerusalem and the Temple, which took place forty years later on August 10, AD 70.*

Horror beyond Comprehension

When judgment prophecies are fulfilled, they bring with them horror beyond comprehension. The destruction of Jerusalem was emblematic of this sort of suffering. In my book *The Eternal Church*, I describe some of the destruction brought on by that judgment:

> The horrors that took place before and after the fall of the city are beyond comprehension. There was murder, rape, and theft such as stealing each other's last morsel of food. Josephus, the great historian, relates a story that was typical of the things that happened to those in the siege who did not take Christ's prophetic words seriously or heed God's opportune time and flee the city, as all the Christians had done. One Mary, the daughter of Eliezar, illustrious for her family and riches, who, being stripped and plundered of all her goods and provisions by the Jewish soldiers [defending the city], in hunger, rage, and despair, killed and boiled her own suckling child, and had eaten one half of him before it was discovered.
>
> Even the Roman general Titus acknowledged that God had helped him to execute God's judgment upon the Jews. When he was viewing the fortifications after the taking of the city, he could not help ascribing his success to God. He made the following statement: "We have fought with God on our side; and it is God who pulled the Jews out of the stronghold: for what could machines or the hands of men avail against such towers as these?" Josephus calculates that over 1.1 million Jews perished in the city, that another 257,660 were killed in surrounding

---

* According to the ancient Jewish historian Josephus, the Temple fell on the ninth of the Jewish month Av, which many scholars correlate to August 10 of that year.

areas, and 97,000 were taken captive. Those above 17 years of age were sent to the works in Egypt; but most were distributed among the Roman provinces, to be destroyed by the sword and by wild beasts as they were forced to fight as gladiators in the amphitheaters. Titus, their conqueror, had 2500 Jews murdered in honor of his brother's birthday, and had a greater number murdered in honor of his father's.

During the destruction of Jerusalem, the temple caught on fire, causing the gold to run into the lower wall and between the blocks of the foundation. The soldiers took the temple apart stone by stone to retrieve the precious metals. There was not one stone left upon another, thus fulfilling the prophecy Jesus gave in Matthew 24:2 and Luke 19:44, which more clearly manifested the fact that God's headquarters was no longer in the law and tabernacle of Moses, or in the great Temple made of stone and precious metals, but now it was in Christ's Church built with lively stones of redeemed mankind.[*]

I share this to show the seriousness of recognizing God's times and seasons of restoration and reformation and of properly responding to the visitation of God they bring. In chapter 1, I explained when and where God fought His World War I and the purpose it fulfilled. We also covered World War II and what God accomplished during that five-hundred-year war for the restoration of the Church. For the rest of this book, we will concentrate on what God will accomplish through His Church during God's World War III.

As I wrote in chapter 1, the saints of God are on the cusp of a great move of God in which they will serve as warriors in a divinely initiated war. God has been preparing His chosen warriors and military officers through intensified testing, training and equipping in weapons and strategy suitable to World War

---

[*] Dr. Bill Hamon, *The Eternal Church*, rev. ed. (Shippensburg, Pa.: Destiny Image, 2003), 80–82.

III. This has been taking place in an accelerated way over the last seven years for the purpose of transitioning His Church army from the moment of declaration of war to the activation of God's offensive. The seven years from 2008 to 2015 were like Israel's seven-day march around Jericho—they were a time of intense training for God's warriors and officers. In relation to Israel's journey from Egypt to possessing the Promised Land, the Church presently stands before the walls of "Jericho": They have now entered their military conquest, and they will not stop until they possess their promised inheritance.

The war will not end until the kingdoms of this world come under the rule of King Jesus and His victorious saints—the point at which the third Church Reformation will be fulfilled. Later I will cover the final battle that will decisively win the war, as described in Revelation 19, and transition the Church to rule and reign with Christ on "a new earth in which righteousness dwells" (2 Peter 3:13).

Now is the time when saints *must* know their weapons of war and how to use them, which is one of the major reasons the Holy Spirit pressed me to write this book. Pastors and all fivefold ministers must now function as drill sergeants and generals to diligently train the saints to be soldiers who know how to fight as warriors: "You therefore must endure hardship [of intensified military training] as a good *soldier* of Jesus Christ. No one engaged in *warfare* entangles himself with the affairs of this life, that he may please him who enlisted him as a *soldier*" (2 Timothy 2:3–4).

Put on the Armor of Light

Several years ago I was ministering with another prophet, Mahesh Chavda. When we finished ministering that night, most everyone was on the floor, "out" in the Spirit (having fallen to the floor under the Spirit's power). We sat on the floor ourselves and started ministering to one another, and the power of God hit us both, laying *us* both out flat.

During the thirty minutes that followed, God gave me a major vision with three different scenes and themes, one of which relates to what we are now discussing. In the vision, a great object like a blimp came and hovered just over my head. The Lord instructed me to use my hands to make an opening in its hull. I reached up and made an opening about two feet long and a foot wide. He instructed me to stretch my hand up into the opening. When I did, a liquid gel began to flow down, covering every inch of my body. When it finished, I had a clear substance about an inch thick covering my entire body. God then instructed me to reach up and make the opening bigger. This time a brilliant light with heat began to penetrate the covering on my body. It made the gel-like substance hard and clearer than crystal, and it began to glow with the brightness of the sun.

The Lord told me the substance was His gold from the New Jerusalem—clear as crystal, representing the robe of righteousness that He had clothed me with. The brilliance of the covering was my *armor of light*. Though the covering was harder than steel, it was still flexible and did not hinder my ability to use any of my senses. I could see, breathe and talk freely. Jesus said, *I am preparing you for the dangerous ministry that I have destined you to fulfill for My Church and Kingdom. This pure-gold, righteous covering will protect you from all the weapons that Satan will seek to use against you. He knows you are a general in My army and that you will help Me raise up a godly army that will defeat his evil kingdom and destroy his reign on earth. Your armor of light can penetrate the darkest hordes of hell and scatter them as light scatters darkness. You will never be defeated as long as you walk in My light and life and keep your light bright—by keeping your battery fully charged by praying in your spirit language.*

Another scene in this vision I described in more detail in chapter 1. Briefly, Jesus introduced me to the archangel Michael as one of His generals over His army of warrior saints. Jesus introduced General Michael to me as His top general over His army of war angels. Jesus said He had committed His heavenly armies to co-labor with and assist His saints in their battles, because He is the Commander in Chief of both armies.

God's Command to His Warrior Saints

Every time God challenged one of His people to do something for Him, He always told them something along these lines: "Fear not! Do not be afraid, fearful or terrified! Do not become fainthearted." This means do not lose spirit or hope or become overly discouraged. God expects us to know Him well enough that we believe He will do everything He promised. God expects us to know He is all powerful, and when we are working with Almighty God to fulfill His purpose, all things are possible!

In fact, angels are shocked at mankind when they do not believe and trust God. God Himself becomes angry, sometimes furious, when He answers our prayers and then, when the next challenge comes up, we question whether God can meet that need. Notice that the biblical record reveals this reality:

> [The children of Israel] tested God in their heart by asking for the food of their fancy. Yes, they spoke against God: They said, "*Can God* prepare a table in the wilderness? Behold, He struck the rock, so that the waters gushed out, and the streams overflowed. *Can He* give bread also? *Can He* provide meat for His people?" Therefore the LORD heard this and was *furious*; so a fire was kindled against Jacob, and anger also came up against Israel, *because they did not believe in God, and did not trust in His salvation.* . . . How often they provoked Him in the wilderness, and grieved Him in the desert! Yes, again and again

they tempted God, and limited the Holy One of Israel. They did not remember His power.

Psalm 78:18–22, 40–42

Scriptures like these make us contemplate whether in our thinking and praying we are saying, *Can God?* versus *God can!* What is God hearing us say? What kind of response are we causing Him to have toward us? Whether we are questioning, "Can God?" or proclaiming, "God can!" determines the warrior spirit. Are we making God smile with pleasure because we consistently trust Him regardless of the challenges? Are we causing a frown on God's face and anger and fury in His heart? Can we provoke God into being angry with us? Yes—"They tested and provoked the Most High God" (verse 56).

Jehovah God, Our Great Equalizer

In Deuteronomy 7, God charges Israel through Moses concerning seven major nations in the land of Canaan that they were to conquer and destroy:

> When the LORD your God brings you into the land which you go to possess, and has cast out many nations before you, the Hittites and the Girgashites and the Amorites and the Canaanites and the Perizzites and the Hivites and the Jebusites, *seven nations greater and mightier than you*, and when the LORD your God delivers them over to you, you shall conquer them and utterly destroy them. You shall make no covenant with them nor show mercy to them.
>
> Deuteronomy 7:1–2

These seven nations represent the seven mountains of culture on the earth today. The Church Kingdom has the same challenge from the Lord Jesus to conquer these mountains and make them subject to the mountain of God, which is to rule over the seven mountains:

> Now it shall come to pass in the latter days that the mountain of the LORD's house shall be established on the top of the mountains, and shall be exalted above the hills; and all nations shall flow to it. Many people shall come and say, "Come, and let us go up to the mountain of the LORD."
>
> Isaiah 2:2–3

God conveyed to the Israelites throughout the book of Deuteronomy that the land of Canaan, which He had chosen for them for their inheritance, was full of millions of people who had been there for generations. They had built great and fortified cities; they were mighty warriors; it was the place where the giants lived. The children of Israel had been slaves for four hundred years, and they were not seasoned warriors. That is the reason God declared that the "-ites" of Canaan were greater and mightier than Israel. But God also conveyed that they should not be concerned about those facts, for God Himself was going to personally fight for Israel against their fierce opponents. That would make Jehovah God *the great equalizer*.

The apostle Paul gave the Church the same assurance: "If God is for us, who can be against us?" (Romans 8:31). Jesus promised His mature Church that none of the plans and demons of hell could prevail against His saintly warriors, nor withstand the warfare of the Church. Why not? Because Jesus has pledged Himself to fight for His Church as Father God promised to fight for His chosen people, Israel.

Notice that all of these promises of God to fight with Israel against their enemies mainly applied to when they entered Canaan and began waging war to dispossess their enemies and possess their Promised Land. Moses told them they were not called to just wander in the wilderness, eat the free manna from heaven and enjoy the shade of the cloud by day and the light and warmth of the fire by night. They were called to accomplish the ultimate purpose of God. God brought them *out*, supernaturally keeping them during the wilderness, in order to take them *in* to go to war and possess the land that God had promised to Abraham and his descendants: "Then He brought us *out* from there, that He might bring us *in*, to give us the land of which He swore to our fathers" (Deuteronomy 6:23).

Today, too many Christians have limited thinking concerning why God saved them. Many think that all God wants to do is bring them out of the world of sin, take them through their wilderness journey in this world and bring them to their Promised Land in heaven. Their purpose in life, they think, is go to church, eat the free manna, soak in the light and warmth of the fire of God and be refreshed in the shadow of His cloud, enjoying the light and wind of His presence. This is somewhat okay in the wilderness, but there is an end to the season of wilderness for the Church and a time to enter in and engage in warfare to fulfill God's ultimate purpose for his mortal Church. This will be accomplished by Jesus and His warriors during God's World War III.

Thank God we have been saved out of sin and are journeying to our heavenly home with our Lord Jesus Christ. We have a war to win first, however, just as the Israelites did, before we fully inherit our new heavens and new earth. The final battle will take place according to Revelation 19, when Jesus as King of kings leads His army of saints against all the wicked of the earth and all religions that are anti-Jesus. If these things happen in the order in which they are written, then the accomplished war in chapter 19 will activate General Michael to bind Satan in the bottomless pit, after which the first resurrection will take place (see Revelation 20:4–6). The translated and resurrected saints then get to reign with Christ for a thousand years on a new earth (see 2 Peter 3:13).

We do not know how all this will be accomplished, but we do know it is on God's agenda and written in His book. We do not have to know all the hows and wheres and whens, but we must believe *God can* accomplish His purpose through us and fulfill His every prophetic decree. We are to make the proper preparation, and Jesus will grant the power and wisdom we will need at that time to fulfill His ultimate plan. At present we apostles and prophets do not understand how all this will work, no more than the twelve apostles knew where, when and how Jesus was going to birth and build His Church. Nevertheless, they were obeying His word to prepare for it and to participate in its birth and co-labor with Christ Jesus in building it. We will do the same in God's World War III. I personally have worked for 64 years co-laboring with Jesus in bringing restoration to His Church—which was the purpose for God's World War II— and I have dedicated the rest of my time on earth to be one of God's generals in the next war and a Third-Reformation reformer in fulfilling Jesus' ultimate purpose for His Church.

The Serious Business of Going to War

I have heard "Be sure your sin will find you out" quoted as Scripture all of my Christian life. But I did not know the biblical setting for it or the motivation that led to its writing. I had always heard it used to bring conviction on people so that they would confess and forsake their hidden sins. It was not until I started searching out all the Scriptures on warfare that I discovered the story behind it and what motivated God to include it in the Bible.

Numbers 32 records the setting for this warning. After Israel had defeated all of the Amorites on the east side of the Jordan, the tribes of Reuben and Gad came to Moses with a request: They wanted to settle in the area east of the Jordan

River, as it was prime land for raising their many cattle, sheep and other livestock. They would not cross over the Jordan to gain an inheritance but allow their inheritance to remain on the east side. At this point, however, the other tribes could not take their promised inheritance, because none of the Israelites' enemies dwelling there had yet been destroyed or driven out of the land.

Moses' response was stern:

> *Shall your brethren go to war while you sit here?* Now why will you discourage the heart of the children of Israel from going over into the land which the LORD has given them? Thus your fathers did when I sent them away from Kadesh Barnea to see the land. For when they went up to the Valley of Eshcol and saw the land, they discouraged the heart of the children of Israel, so that they did not go into the land which the LORD had given them. So the LORD's anger was aroused on that day, and He swore an oath, saying, "Surely none of the men who came up from Egypt, from twenty years old and above, shall see the land of which I swore to Abraham, Isaac, and Jacob, because they have not wholly followed Me. . . ." So the LORD's anger was aroused against Israel, and He made them wander in the wilderness forty years, until all the generation that had done evil in the sight of the LORD was gone. And look! You have risen in your fathers' place, a brood of sinful men, to increase still more the fierce anger of the LORD against Israel. For if you turn away from following Him, He will once again leave them in the wilderness, and you will destroy all these people.
>
> Numbers 32:6–15

At this, the tribes assured Moses that they intended to do no such thing; rather, once settling their families in the land they had chosen for themselves, they would join their armed brothers in driving the Canaanites out of the land God had sworn to give them:

We will build sheepfolds here for our livestock, and cities for
our little ones, but we ourselves will be armed, ready to go
before the children of Israel until we have brought them to
their place; and our little ones will dwell in the fortified cities
because of the inhabitants of the land. We will not return to
our homes until every one of the children of Israel has received
his inheritance.

Verses 16–18

Moses gave his assent, but in his response to the tribes of Reuben and Gad, notice God's attitude concerning those who
would quit fighting before the war is won for everyone:

Then Moses said to them: "*If* you do this thing, *if* you *arm
yourselves* before the LORD for the *war*, and all your armed men
cross over the Jordan before the LORD until He has driven out
His enemies from before Him, and the land is subdued before
the LORD, then afterward you may return and be blameless
before the LORD and before Israel; and this land shall be your
possession before the LORD. *But if you do not do so, then take
note, you have sinned against the LORD; and be sure your sin
will find you out.*"

Verses 20–23

Remember that everything God spoke to the children of Israel concerning their war in Canaan has application for the
Church in God's World War III. The book of Joshua is like a
training manual on fighting and winning the war. The book of
Deuteronomy, meanwhile, is the instruction manual that gives
principles for this war. Study these books thoroughly in order
to be a greater warrior and officer in God's World War III.

As a warrior, obedient to your Commander in Chief, do not
say in your heart, "These nations are greater than I; how can I
dispossess them?" (Deuteronomy 7:17). But *do* this: .

You shall not be terrified of them; for the LORD your God, the great and awesome God, is among you. And the LORD your God will drive out those nations before you little by little; you will be unable to destroy them at once, lest the beasts of the field become too numerous for you. But *the LORD your God will* deliver them over to you, and will inflict defeat upon them until they are destroyed. And *He will* deliver their kings into your hand, and *you will* destroy their name from under heaven; no one shall be able to stand against you *until you have destroyed them.*

Verses 21–24

ENLIGHTENMENT, DECLARATION AND PRAYER

Father God, in Jesus' name I ask that You make sure I do not miss my day of visitation, as the Israelite leaders did. I declare that I am a warrior and soldier of Jesus Christ, clothed with the whole armor of God. Your World Wars I and II were before my time, but now is the time of Your World War III. Jesus, I volunteer to be in Your army and acknowledge You as my Commander in Chief. I know some of my enemies are greater warriors than I, but You are my great equalizer. I will go with You into battle unafraid, knowing that You are greater and more powerful than all my enemies.

5

Jesus, Lord of Heaven's Armies

Before we can talk about the Church doing corporate warfare against the evil forces of Satan, we must be convinced that our God is a warrior and fights for His people. In the previous chapters we showed that God created mankind to be His special people. They would be His kind of people, made in His own image and likeness. God desired to be identified with the human race. He did not want to create a special body for Jesus, the way He did for Adam. He loved the body He made for man, and He wanted His Son to have such a body. And He wanted to use the method He empowered man and woman to use to produce that human body. This would fulfill two desires of God: First, it would fulfill the eternal nature and desire of Father God to have a biological Son. By the procreative power of His Holy Spirit, He impregnated a young virgin woman who birthed a human body that God fathered. This then fulfilled Father God's second desire, for His Son to have a beautiful human body.

Jesus, Son of Man—Christ, Son of God

The archangel Gabriel told Mary to name that body Jesus. He would be known in heaven and earth as Christ, Son of God, and Jesus, Son of man. When scriptural reference is made to the name *Jesus*, it always refers to the personal life and body of Jesus. That is the reason the Bible never says that we have Jesus in us or that the Church is the Body of Jesus. It states that we have *Christ* in us and the Church is the Body of *Christ*. The Greek word for Christ, *Christos*, means "anointed." The name *Jesus* reveals Him as Son of man; Christ reveals Him as Son of God.

Jesus was both human and divine, man and God, mortal and eternal. He became God's perfect man and man's perfect God. Through His Son, Jesus, Father God joined the human race by becoming one of them. God is not a respecter of persons, but He does take sides in the human race. For those who follow Him, becoming His type among mankind, God will fight for them against other human beings who reject God and His way of living. For those humans who become so corrupt that they defile humanity and the earth that God created, He has no qualms or restraint about destroying them in the same way He destroyed the ungodly, wicked generation preceding the Flood.

All God-fearing, conscientious Christians want to know something is scriptural and find examples in the Bible that demonstrate how the Scriptures are applied before they accept it as divine truth. So let us examine several Scriptures and biblical examples that show our God is a warrior who fights against people and nations that come against His people.

Commander in Chief of God's Army

Let us first take note that in the Bible there are 240 references to God as the Lord of Hosts. *Hosts* refers to a group of people prepared for war. In some translations this term is rendered "Lord of heaven's armies." Before Joshua could lead God's people into the land of Canaan to destroy the nations there—31 kings and their armies—he had to have a revelation of God as Commander in Chief of the armies of heaven and of the Israelite army Joshua was about to lead in the campaign to conquer and possess Canaan.

> And it came to pass, when Joshua was by Jericho, that he lifted his eyes and looked, and behold, a Man stood opposite him with His sword drawn in His hand. And Joshua went to Him and said to Him, "Are You for us or for our adversaries?" So He said, "No, but as *Commander of the army of the* LORD I have now come." And Joshua fell on his face to the earth and worshiped, and said to Him, "What does my Lord say to His servant?" Then the *Commander of the* LORD's *army* said to Joshua, "Take your sandal off your foot, for the place where you stand is holy."
>
> Joshua 5:13–15

We know this heavenly being was not an angel like Michael, the top general in God's angelic army, for every time an angel appeared to a man and the man tried to worship him, the angel forbade it. But this person, the Commander in Chief of the army of the Lord, accepted the worship. Theologians call it a *theophany*, which is a manifestation of God in human form. It is an appearance of Christ before He came to earth to take on a human body. Today He is the same Commander in Chief of the Lord's army—Jesus Christ.

Scriptures Revealing a Warrior God

A careful reading of the Bible turns up many Scriptures that describe God as one who fights and makes war; in many cases (as I mentioned above), He is called the Lord of Hosts. Let's survey just a sample of these Scriptures, with the key words emphasized.

A God Who Fights

Joshua conquered all the land [of Canaan] . . . because the LORD God of Israel *fought* for Israel.

Joshua 10:40, 42

One man of you shall chase a thousand, for the LORD your God is He who *fights* for you.

Joshua 23:10

The LORD your God is with you . . . who goes with you, to *fight* for you against your enemies.

Deuteronomy 20:1, 4

The LORD your God, who goes before you, He will *fight* for you.

Deuteronomy 1:30

You must not fear them, for the LORD *your God Himself fights* for you.

Deuteronomy 3:22

Do not be afraid. . . . *the* LORD *will fight* for you.

Exodus 14:13–14

With us is the LORD *our God*, to help us and to *fight our battles*.

2 Chronicles 32:8

Our *God will fight* for us.

Nehemiah 4:20

The Lord of Hosts

When people in Old Testament times called upon God by the name Lord of Hosts, they did it deliberately because they needed God to act mightily on their behalf. When King Hezekiah prayed to the Lord of Hosts to deliver him from the great Assyrian army in Isaiah 37:16, God sent one of His war angels to kill 185,000 Assyrian warriors in one night (see verse 36). When the Scriptures talk about the Lord of Hosts doing certain things, they refer to God with His war angels and warrior saints accomplishing what needs to be done.

The *zeal* of the LORD *of hosts* shall do this.

2 Kings 19:31

I [David] come to you in the name of the LORD *of hosts*, the God of the armies of Israel, whom you have defied.

1 Samuel 17:45

Behold, the Lord, the LORD *of hosts*, will lop off the bough with terror; those of high stature will be hewn down, and the haughty will be humbled.

Isaiah 10:33

The LORD *of hosts* musters the *army* for *battle*.

Isaiah 13:4

The LORD *of hosts* has purposed, and who will annul it?

Isaiah 14:27

The Commander of the armies of heaven has done it to destroy your pride and show his contempt for all the greatness of mankind.

Isaiah 23:9 TLB

75

In that day the LORD of hosts will be for a crown of glory and a diadem of beauty to the remnant of His people.

Isaiah 28:5

But, O LORD of hosts, You who test the righteous, and see the mind and heart, let me see Your vengeance on them; for I have pleaded my cause before You.

Jeremiah 20:12 (see also 11:20)

Thus says the LORD of hosts, the God of Israel: "Behold, I will punish the king of Babylon and his land, as I have punished the king of Assyria."

Jeremiah 50:18

"For My name shall be great among the nations," says the Lord of hosts.

Malachi 1:11

So a book of remembrance was written before Him for those who fear the Lord and who meditate on His name. "They shall be Mine," says the LORD of hosts, "on the day that I make them My jewels. And I will spare them as a man spares his own son who serves him."

Malachi 3:16–17

"For behold, the day is coming, burning like an oven, and all the proud, yes, all who do wickedly will be stubble. And the day which is coming shall burn them up," says the LORD of hosts, "That will leave them neither root nor branch. But to you who fear My name, the Sun of Righteousness shall arise with healing in His wings; and you shall go out and grow fat like stall-fed calves. You shall trample the wicked, for they shall be ashes under the soles of your feet on the day that I do this," says the LORD of hosts.

Malachi 4:1–3

Malachi 3:10 shares one other thing that the Lord of Hosts will do: He will open the windows of heaven for tithe payers. If you practice tithing, I want to encourage you that the Lord of Hosts Himself is fighting for you, clearing the way for you to have an open heaven.

God of War

Who is this King of glory? The LORD *strong and mighty*, the LORD *mighty in battle*. . . . The LORD *of Hosts*, He is the King of glory.

Psalm 24:8, 10

The LORD is a man of war.

Exodus 15:3

War broke out in heaven: Michael and his angels *fought* with the dragon [Satan].

Revelation 12:7

The LORD will have *war* with Amalek from generation to generation.

Exodus 17:16

They made *war*. . . . They cried out to God in the *battle*. He heeded their prayer, because they put their trust in Him. . . . Many [of their enemies] fell dead, because the *war* was God's.

1 Chronicles 5:19–20, 22

Blessed be the LORD my Rock, who trains my hands for *war*, and my fingers for battle.

Psalm 144:1, of David the warrior

To everything there is a season, a time for every purpose under heaven . . . a time of *war* . . .

Ecclesiastes 3:1, 8

The LORD shall go forth like a mighty man; He shall stir up His *zeal* like a *man of war*.

Isaiah 42:13

Prepare for *war*! Wake up the mighty men, let all the *men of war* draw near, let them come up. Beat your plowshares into swords and your pruning hooks into spears; let the weak say, "I am strong." . . . Cause Your mighty ones to go down there, O LORD.

Joel 3:9–11

The LORD gives voice before *His army*, for His camp is very great; for strong is the One who executes His word.

Joel 2:11

The same horn was making *war* against the saints, and prevailing against them, until the Ancient of Days came, and a judgment was made in favor of the saints of the Most High, and the time came for the saints to possess the kingdom.

Daniel 7:21–22

We do not *war* according to the flesh. For the weapons of our warfare are not carnal but mighty in God for pulling down [satanic] strongholds.

2 Corinthians 10:3–4

These will make *war* with the Lamb, and the Lamb will overcome them, for He is Lord of lords and King of kings; and those who are *with Him* are *called, chosen, and faithful*.

Revelation 17:14

He who overcomes, and keeps My works until the end, to him I will give power over the nations—"He [the overcomer] shall rule them [the nations] with a rod of iron; they shall be dashed to pieces like the potter's vessels"—as I [Jesus] also have received from My Father.

Revelation 2:26–27

If any doubt remains that God violently confronts the enemies of His saints—or that those who rebel against Him meet a terrible end—consider carefully the description of Jesus in Revelation 19, when He comes to exact the judgment of God upon the nations:

Now I saw heaven opened, and behold, a white horse. And He who sat on him was called Faithful and True, and in righteousness He judges and makes *war*. His eyes were like a flame of fire, and on His head were many crowns. He had a name written that no one knew except Himself. He was clothed with a robe dipped in blood, and His name is called The Word of God. And the *armies in heaven*, clothed in fine linen, white and clean, followed Him on white horses. Now out of His mouth goes a sharp sword, that with it He should strike the nations. And He Himself will rule them with a rod of iron. He Himself treads the winepress of the fierceness and wrath of Almighty God. And He has on His robe and on His thigh a name written: King of kings and Lord of lords. . . .

I saw the beast, the kings of the earth, and their *armies*, gathered together to make *war* against Him who sat on the horse and against *His army*. Then the beast was captured, and with him the false prophet who worked signs in his presence, by which he deceived those who received the mark of the beast and those who worshiped his image. These two were cast alive into the lake of fire burning with brimstone. And the rest were killed with the sword which proceeded from the mouth of Him who sat on the horse. And all the birds were filled with their flesh.

Revelation 19:11–16, 19–21

Christian overcomers will be joint heirs with Christ Jesus and receive the same commission to rule and reign over things of the new earth along with Jesus. We know the armies on the white horses with Jesus are not angels but saints, for those with King Jesus, whose robe was dipped in blood, are clothed in fine linen; this matches the description of the Bride of Christ, who in verse 8 is clothed in fine linen, clean and bright, for the fine linen is the righteous acts of the saints.

Does God Personally Fight?

In Joshua 10 we read an illustration of God personally fighting with His own hands and killing human enemies. Let us look at the incidents that led to this great battle. God commanded Joshua to destroy every human being in the land of Canaan. This was in accordance with Genesis 15:16, in which God prophesied the return of Abraham's descendants to the land, which could only happen once the iniquity of the Amorites was complete. Evidently, that time had come; the sin of the Amorites was now full enough for God to execute His judgments upon them.

The "-ites" of Canaan had reached a tipping point. This was a grave situation, for God had already demonstrated that when any part of the human race reaches a certain tipping point in their corrupt and evil ways, God activates His judgments. When the pre-Flood generation reached that tipping point, God destroyed them. In Genesis 18–19, we read that the Lord came down to earth to check out the report that Sodom and Gomorrah had reached that stage of wickedness. The following Scriptures reveal God's conclusion of the situation and the action He took:

> And the LORD said, Because the cry of Sodom and Gomorrah is great, and because their sin is very grievous; I will go down

80

now, and see whether they have done altogether according to the cry of it, which is come unto me; and if not, I will know. . . .

Then the LORD rained upon Sodom and upon Gomorrah brimstone and fire from the LORD out of heaven; and he overthrew those cities, and all the plain, and all the inhabitants of the cities, and that which grew upon the ground.

Genesis 18:20–21; 19:24–25 KJV

God the eternal judge proclaimed all in the land of Canaan guilty and sentenced them to death. Joshua and several hundred thousand of his warriors were appointed to be executioners of the condemned.

Seven of the major nations in Canaan were named and condemned to total annihilation; the Amorites were the most powerful and ungodly of these. Most of the giants came from their nation. As the Israelites began to rack up military victories, the Hittites heard how Joshua's God was helping him destroy every army he came against. Residents of the Hittite capital, Gibeon, feared for their lives, so they devised a plan to make peace with Joshua by convincing him that they were not from Canaan. They successfully deceived Joshua into believing their story. They were able to do this because Israel "did not ask counsel of the LORD" (Joshua 9:14). As a result, Joshua made a covenant with them that they would not be killed.

When the five Amorite kings of northern Canaan heard that Gibeon had made a peace covenant with Israel, they grew very concerned. Gibeon was a great city where the national army was stationed, and all their soldiers were fierce warriors. The kings decided to attack and kill the Gibeonites before they joined forces with Israel. They assembled their five armies, hundreds of thousands of warriors. When the Gibeonites discovered it, they sent a message to Joshua at his headquarters at Gilgal to come immediately to help them. Here is the biblical account of what happened next:

81

So Joshua ascended from Gilgal, he and all the people of war with him, and all the mighty men of valor. And the LORD said to Joshua, "Do not fear them, for I have delivered them into your hand; not a man of them shall stand before you." Joshua therefore came upon them suddenly, having marched all night from Gilgal.

Joshua 10:7–9

These warriors were like U.S. Marines! After marching all night they immediately engaged in the battle and fought all day. Here is how the battle went:

So the LORD routed them before Israel, killed them with a great slaughter at Gibeon, chased them along the road that goes to Beth Horon, and struck them down as far as Azekah and Makkedah. And it happened, as they fled before Israel and were on the descent of Beth Horon, that *the LORD cast down large hailstones from heaven on them* as far as Azekah, *and they died. There were more who died from the hailstones than the children of Israel killed with the sword.*

Then Joshua spoke to the LORD in the day when the LORD delivered up the Amorites before the children of Israel, and he said in the sight of Israel: "Sun, stand still over Gibeon; and Moon, in the Valley of Aijalon." So the sun stood still, and the moon stopped, till the people had revenge upon their enemies. . . . So the sun stood still in the midst of heaven, and did not hasten to go down for about a whole day. There has been no day like that, before it or after it, that the LORD heeded the voice of a man; for *the LORD fought for Israel.*

Joshua 10:10–14

Let me dramatize what happened, the way I do when I preach, so you can more perfectly visualize the scene. Hailstones are among God's weapons of war stored in His armory, as He said to Job: "Have you seen the treasury of hail, which I have reserved for the time of trouble, for the day of battle and war?" (Job 38:22–23). Let us view Joshua's battle from God's vantage point: The Lord of the armies of heaven and His leading general, Michael, are watching the unfolding battle. His man Joshua and Joshua's multitude of warriors are killing Amorites right and left. God says to Michael, "Look at my mighty warrior Joshua. Look how fiercely and valiantly he is fighting. He is doing exactly what I commanded, executing my judgments upon the Amorites." As God watches, He gets excited about the battle and says to His general, "Go to my armory and bring me some of those hailstone bombs. I have to get into this battle!" Michael brings him an armload of ice bombs, and God yells down to Joshua, "Hey, there are five hundred escaping over that hill. But it's all right—don't be concerned, because I will take care of them." He drops a hailstone bomb in the midst of the five hundred, and they are blown to pieces. He sees about a thousand trying to come around behind Joshua's warriors, so He throws three hailstone bombs, and a thousand Amorite warriors are killed. And so it continues throughout the day.

And this was no ordinary day. Joshua commanded the sun to stand still and the moon not to move until he had killed all of his enemies, and they stood still for almost another day. This gave the Israelites at least ten extra hours of daylight, which they used to kill more of their enemies. When Joshua gave this command to the heavens, God had to take a few minutes to command the entire solar system, perhaps the entire Milky Way galaxy, to stop rotating without losing its gravitational functions. It was the greatest miracle in the universe, and it happened to give Joshua and God extra time to kill more of their enemies. They fought the entirety of that extra-long day until all the Amorites were destroyed.

Then God told the Holy Spirit to make sure, when He inspired Joshua to record this battle, to reveal to him how God had personally fought in the battle and to make sure it was recorded for all to read: More died from the hailstone bombs that God threw than all the people Joshua and his army killed with the sword. "I want the world to know that I am the mightiest of all warriors," He was saying, "the King of kings and the Lord of lords. I am a mighty warrior who fights for My people and enables them to kill human enemies." Is that just my overactive imagination? No! The battle was probably more dramatic than we have words to express. Be assured that God is a mighty warrior and is committed to fighting for us in His World War III.

Let us lay hold of the charge that Joshua gave his captains after they had won the war and captured the five kings. He had all of his captains come one by one and place their feet on the necks of these kings. Joshua said to them the same thing that our Mighty Warrior, Jesus Christ, is saying to us today about our opposition: "Do not be afraid, nor be dismayed; be strong and of good courage, for thus the LORD will do to all your enemies against whom you fight" (verse 25).

God's Sovereignty versus Our Participation

God's desire and purpose is to work with His people on earth. There are a few incidents in the Bible where it appears that God did something on earth sovereignly by Himself without human participation; on closer examination, however, we find that mankind is involved. God rarely (if ever) does anything on earth without a person being involved. When God created man, He told him that earth was his area of dominion. God gave man authority over everything on earth. He even told Adam that he could name all the animals, birds and fish; whatever name he gave them, heaven and earth would recognize them by that name.

In order to bring redemption to man, God did not send an angel or some other heavenly being; He did not even come

Himself as God almighty. He sent His Son to become a mortal man. It would require a *man*, the sinless Son of God, to provide redemption for mankind.

When God appeared to Gideon, He told him that He had chosen Gideon to be the one to deliver Israel from the rule and oppression of the Midianites: "Then the LORD turned to [Gideon] and said, 'Go in this might of yours, and *you shall* save Israel from the hand of the Midianites. Have I not sent you?'" (Judges 6:14). When God spoke to Moses to commission him to deliver God's people from bondage, He gave Moses seven promises, covering everything from bringing the people out of Egypt to taking them into their Promised Land. Each promise began with God saying, "*I will*." Be assured that whether God commissions you with "You will" or "I will," He means, "We will." We cannot do His work without Him, and He will not do it without us. All of God's activity on the earth will directly or indirectly involve His people in some way or another.

Judgment on the Wicked

Everything God does on earth is because of man, for man and with man to accomplish His purposes for man and earth. We must face the fact that the Bible records God killing millions of people and enabling His people to kill millions of people. I am sharing this to show God's intricate involvement in the human race—to show God's attitude about and actions concerning the death of the wicked. God loves mankind and wants them to be the way He made them to be, but when they corrupt their ways, rebelling against God by their attitudes and actions, then they are not God's type of humans and are fit only for destruction.

The Flood (Genesis 6:1–8:22). God sent water from the sky and from underneath the earth to drown all the people on earth. God did, however, preserve the human race by commissioning Noah to build the Ark. God does with His almighty power what man cannot do, but He always has a person on earth participating in the process.

God's judgments on Egypt (Exodus 6:26–15:3). God did what the man Moses could not do in sending the ten plagues on Egypt and dividing the Red Sea so that God's people could escape. In so doing, God destroyed the Egyptian army by releasing the waters He had been holding back. God did some sovereign acts, but Moses and the children of Israel had a significant part to play, too.

Destruction of Sodom and Gomorrah (Genesis 18:20–19:29). God sovereignly rained fire and brimstone on these cities, executing God's judgment against their perversion, wickedness and ungodliness. But God had first checked with His friend Abraham, allowing him to negotiate for the cities before executing His judgment upon them. Lot and his family had to be taken out before God's wrath was poured out on the wicked cities.

Defeat and destruction of the Assyrians (Isaiah 36–37). God sent one of His powerful war angels to kill 185,000 Assyrian soldiers. This was in response to the intercessory prayer of King Hezekiah and the prophecy of Isaiah.

God did not shy away from killing those ungodly people. Look at the numbers destroyed: Twenty million of all ages killed in the great Flood. Perhaps five hundred thousand Egyptians were killed in the plagues, including the firstborn of every family and two hundred thousand foot soldiers, six thousand charioteers and twelve hundred horses who drowned in the Red Sea. Joshua and his army killed approximately three million people in Canaan. And millions were killed when God helped David and the succeeding righteous kings in their wars over the next thousand years. These enemies of God were real people—dads, moms, children. In the Christian age, we as God's spiritual people do not fight and kill natural human beings, but we do fight and destroy Satan's evil army of wicked spirits.

Some have asked me if we can kill eternal spirit beings. I do not think so. But we can bind them, neutralize them and deactivate them so that they are no longer effective against us and God's purpose on earth. General Michael and his war angels did not kill Lucifer and the angels that followed him, but they did remove them from a place of influence in heaven and bound them in chains of darkness. The books of Jude and 2 Peter warn Christians that if they turn away from God and start following the ways of the devil, they will suffer the same fate as the once glorious and perfect Lucifer, who turned from the ways of God to his own ways of pride, self-will and rebellion against the rule of the Almighty.

The saints do believe! Many evangelical and some Pentecostal denominations do not teach the reality of spiritual warfare or that God is ever involved in wars or killing certain people. This is not part of their belief system. And yet they will preach that in the last days God and Israel will kill many millions of people when certain nations gather to destroy Israel. They also believe that when Jesus returns, He is going to kill every antichrist person on the earth and cast billions into the lake of fire, which is the second death.

Old Testament God versus New Testament God?

When I teach about these things, some have said to me, "You are talking about the Old Testament God. We serve the New Testament God, who is only merciful and forgiving." My answer is that we do not have two Gods. God is one. The Bible does reveal two covenants (written in two testaments), the Old and the New. But they were put in place by the same God.

Father God wanted to show His nature of love by sending His Son to demonstrate Father God's love for humanity. It was the God of the Old Testament who so loved the world that He gave His only begotten Son that whosoever believes in Jesus should not perish but have everlasting life. We see this in Psalm 22 and Isaiah 53, which reveal the love God had for the human race in the agony and suffering He allowed Jesus to go through to redeem man back to God. The New Testament magnifies God's love and grace. This did not change God's nature, however, for He always remains the same yesterday, today and forever (see Hebrews 13:8). In another place He says, "I am the LORD, I do not change" (Malachi 3:6). In different dispensations we see different manifestations of God's nature and character. Jehovah God was "God is love" always, but it was not until Calvary that He had the opportunity to demonstrate that "God is love" to all of His created beings, both angelic and human.

The Bible declares that grace and truth came by Jesus Christ. Jesus is declared the Son of God, God manifest in the flesh, the door to heaven, the way, the truth, the life, the light of the world, the resurrection and the life and many more. Though Jesus was the love of God made manifest, there is no Scripture that states, "Jesus is love," the way the Bible says, "God is love." We know that Jesus is God's love personified. There is no way through Scripture that anyone can make a difference between Jehovah of the Old Testament and Jesus of the New; whatever the one is, the other is. The true *agape* love that God has always been was not made known until Jesus demonstrated it by dying on the cross and shedding His life's blood for the human race.

The God of the Old is the God of the New. Jesus declared, "I and My Father are one." Christians have historically been divided on many aspects of the Trinity—some believe the God-head is one God in three persons, some that the Godhead is three persons in one God. Others teach that there are three separate Gods in three separate beings that are nevertheless one God in nature, character and being; still others believe that there is one God manifest in one person—Jesus Christ. Regardless of their view of the Godhead, *all* believe there is just one God. We can safely say that whatever God the Father is, Jesus the Son is the same, for Jesus said, "He who has seen Me has seen the Father" (John 14:9). Jesus is "the brightness of His glory and the express image of His person" (Hebrews 1:3). What Jesus is, the Holy Spirit is, and our Holy Spirit language has access to all the attributes of the Godhead. God is a warrior, and that means that Jesus and the Holy Spirit also are. Our Holy Spirit–given spirit language has the warrior nature. The same is true for all the attributes of God.

ENLIGHTENMENT, DECLARATION AND PRAYER

Jesus, all the Scriptures referenced in this chapter reveal to me that You are a mighty warrior and You personally fight for Your people. I am thankful to be one of Your people. You are the Lord of Hosts, God of the angel armies in heaven. God, I declare that You are just and right when You destroy the wicked who are corrupting Your earth and Your mankind creation. Jesus, give me the same love for righteousness and hatred of all evil as You had when You were here on earth, as it is written in Hebrews 1:9.

6

God's Purpose in Corporate Warfare

We have now examined the scriptural proof that God identifies with the human race and fights for His chosen people against their human enemies. And who exactly is He fighting for? In the Old Testament God set apart a special people for Himself, through whom He could demonstrate to the rest of humanity His identity and His almighty power.

He called Abram (later, Abraham) out of his home country to a special land that God had designated for him and his descendants to inherit as their Promised Land. This inheritance was not immediate but would be worked out for thousands of years. Abraham's part was to move to the land of Canaan, walk its full length and breadth and declare it verbally to be his land according to the promise of God (see Genesis 13:17).

Abraham and Sarah had a son named Isaac. Isaac had a son named Jacob who, with his wives and concubines, had twelve sons. After Jacob's experience wrestling with an angel for the blessing, his name was changed to Israel. His twelve sons became the fathers of the twelve tribes of Israel—referred to throughout the Bible as the children of Israel. Today the modern descendants of these twelve tribes include the Jews of the Diaspora and the nation of Israel (the Israelis).

Why a Special Race?

God was very intentional about raising up a special people, and later a nation, so that it would be reported around the world that they were the people of Jehovah God. He wanted a special people through whom He could demonstrate that Jehovah alone was the almighty God who created the heavens and the earth and the human race. God allowed His people—Jacob and his family, seventy in all—to relocate to Egypt, eventually coming into bondage to the Egyptians, for 430 years. Why would God allow this?

There are at least three reasons.

1. Israel Had to Multiply

Israel would not have been able to possess already-inhabited Canaan as a family of seventy. They had to multiply into a nation of millions, fulfilling part of God's prophecy to Abraham that his seed would multiply like the stars of the sky and the sand of the sea. They needed enough men to make a sufficient army of more than 600,000 and enough people to occupy the land once they had destroyed all its present occupants.

2. God Wanted to Demonstrate His Power

The second reason God allowed His people to be enslaved for 430 years—nearly twice as long as the United States has been a nation—was that God was raising up Egypt as a world empire for the purpose of demonstrating His power against their Pharaoh-god. "For the Scripture says to the Pharaoh, 'For this very purpose I have raised you up, that I may show

My power in you, and that My name may be declared in all the earth'" (Romans 9:17; see also Exodus 9:16). God was concerned about His reputation. He wanted His reputation as the greatest of all gods to spread around the world, especially to the warriors in the land of Canaan. He wanted them to know what kind of God was bringing His people to drive them out of that land.

> But the LORD said to Moses, "Pharaoh will not heed you, so that My wonders may be multiplied in the land of Egypt. . . . Then I will harden Pharaoh's heart, so that he will pursue them; and I will gain honor over Pharaoh and over all his army, that the Egyptians may know that I am the LORD. . . . And I indeed will harden the hearts of the Egyptians, and they shall follow [the Israelites into the divided Red Sea]. So I will gain honor over Pharaoh and over all his army, his chariots, and his horsemen."
>
> Exodus 11:9; 14:4, 17

The terrible mistreatment of God's people as slaves in Egypt gave God more justification for executing His destructive powers on Pharaoh and the Egyptian empire, which was full of false gods and ungodly living.

3. The Canaanites' Sin Was Not Yet Full

There was a third reason Israel could not possess Canaan in Abraham's lifetime:

> Then [God] said to Abram: "Know certainly that your descendants will be strangers in a land that is not theirs, and will serve them, and they will afflict them four hundred years. And also the nation whom they serve I will judge; afterward they shall come out with great possessions. Now as for you, you shall go to your fathers in peace; you shall be buried at a good old

age. But in the fourth generation they shall return here, *for the iniquity of the Amorites is not yet complete.*"

Genesis 15:13–16

The Amorites were the largest nation in Canaan, and we should conclude because of their size, power and influence that they represented to God all the "-ite" nations of Canaan. But until the fourth generation, they would not have sinned enough to reach the tipping point that I discussed in the last chapter.

Progressive Revelation of the Kingdom

God did many things in Israel and with the Israelite people: He brought them out of Egypt through the ten plagues; He parted the Red Sea and did other miracles in the wilderness; He gave them the Ten Commandments, His laws of dos and don'ts; He led Joshua in leading the people in a seven-year military campaign to make the kingdoms of Canaan the kingdom of God's people.

The apostle Paul taught that these accounts were not recorded just to have a written record of Israel's history; all these miracles and wonders *really happened*, and Paul said the Holy Spirit had something in mind that was beyond the natural. He had the Church in mind, which Jesus would purchase by shedding His own life's blood on a cruel cross. He knew that Israel's experiences gave a living illustration of what God's new chosen people, the Church race, would experience in their journey, from origination to ultimate destination: "Now all these things happened to them as examples, and they were written for our admonition, upon whom the ends of the ages have come" (1 Corinthians 10:11). "For whatever things were written before were written for our learning" (Romans 15:4).

In my major book on the Church, *The Eternal Church*, I cover the Church's origin, deterioration, restoration and ultimate destination, all of which are typified by the history of Israel. Abraham's call and entering Canaan to claim it as his own is a type of the origin of the Church. Israel's years of bondage in Egypt portray the Church's bondage to religious dead works during the thousand-year Dark Ages. Israel's experiences in their journey from Egypt to Canaan portray the seven major restoration movements that took place from 1517 to 2007. Joshua and his army beginning their military campaign to dispossess the "-ites" of Canaan is typical of the beginning of God's World War III. It is the first major thrust of the Holy Spirit during the Third Church Reformation that began in 2008.*

We are joint heirs with Christ Jesus and co-warriors with Him to win this final battle. Our victory will bring about the consummation of the ages, destroying all of Christ's enemies and establishing the Kingdom dominion of Jesus and His army-Church over the new earth (see 2 Peter 3:13; Revelation 5:10; 11:15; 20:6). Evidently you are called to be a part of God's end time army, for the Holy Spirit has providentially caused you to be reading this book at this time. Jesus wants you to be an active warrior in His victorious army. You have been going through God's intensified testing and training to prepare you for this day and hour. Keep reading until you discover your part in fulfilling God's end time purpose in and through His Church.

---

* I have written books on the last few Holy Spirit restoration movements, including the prophetic movement (*Prophets and the Prophetic Movement*, Destiny Image, 2001), the apostolic movement (*Apostles, Prophets and the Coming Moves of God*, Destiny Image, 1997), the saints movement (*The Day of the Saints*, Destiny Image, 2002), and the Third Reformation, *Prophetic Scriptures Yet to Be Fulfilled*. Now this book covers what I call the army of the Lord movement.

ENLIGHTENMENT, DECLARATION AND PRAYER

God, You chose Abraham to start the Israelite nation so You could have a people who would be recognized by the nations of the world as God almighty's chosen people. I now understand that You did that to demonstrate Your standard of right living for mankind and to manifest Your mighty power, gaining a reputation among the nations of the world. Jesus, as a member of Your Church, I am one of Your called-out ones. Help me to be a demonstration of who You are and Your mighty power. Let 2 Corinthians 4:7–11 be activated within me until the life of Jesus is being manifest in my mortal flesh and Galatians 2:20 is a reality in my life. Empower me to be a full believer so that I can fulfill Your declarations in John 14:12 and Mark 16:16–18.

7

Corporate Weapons for Warfare

"For though we walk in the flesh," Paul tells us in 2 Corinthians 10:3–4, "we do not war according to the flesh. For the weapons of our warfare are not carnal but mighty in God for pulling down strongholds." If God calls us to go to war, then it is reasonable to believe that He arms us with weapons to fight. But the Scriptures also instruct us to let everything be proved and witnessed by two or three. We have a second scriptural witness in the New Testament that, like the first, emphatically declares that we are in a war and have been given weapons to fight with:

> Finally, my brethren, be strong in the Lord and in the power of His might. Put on the whole armor of God, that you may be able to stand against the wiles of the devil. For we do not wrestle against flesh and blood, but against principalities, against powers, against the rulers of the darkness of this age, against spiritual hosts [armies] of wickedness in the heavenly places.
>
> Ephesians 6:10–12

In addition we have numerous Old Testament examples of God's people taking up their weapons to win the battle.

Some of our weapons are meant to be used in personal battles, and some are designed for corporate battles. Individually we must have on the whole armor of God for both protection and offensive warfare. Offensively, the warrior's armor contains the sword of the Spirit, which is the Word of God. Jesus' first major battle against Satan in the wilderness was won using the sword of the Spirit. We must have Christ in us and rebuke the devil in the name of Jesus.

The helmet of salvation represents our covering by the blood of Jesus. The breastplate of righteousness means our trust is completely in God and our attitude and actions are according to the righteousness of Christ. The belt of truth means we have balanced doctrine and are walking in all presently restored truth. The combat boots mean you are properly prepared to demonstrate the Gospel and ready to march in the army of the Lord. The shield of faith shows you know the Word of God well enough to counteract every false accusation and attack of the enemy.

In addition to these, we can go on the offensive by praying in the spirit language for inner strength and empowerment. Prayer and praise are also weapons of power for the Christian soldier. All of these are necessary to be a victorious Christian who wins battles against every enemy. It helps when the army goes into corporate warfare if all the soldiers are fully clothed with their whole armor.

Corporate Weapons of Mass Destruction

The Scriptures reveal the powerful results produced when saints come together in unity and all do the same thing at the same time. God commands the blessing and the resurrection life of Jesus

Christ to manifest mightily when saints come together in unity to fulfill a purpose of God (see Psalm 133). Leviticus 26:1–8 declares that if Israel would keep all of God's commandments and live according to His way, they would prosper in everything they did and Israel would win their battles against their enemies. "Five of you shall chase a hundred, and a hundred of you shall put ten thousand to flight; your enemies shall fall by the sword before you" (verse 8). Notice that when five soldiers join together to fight, each soldier kills twenty enemies. But when a hundred unify to fight, each soldier kills one hundred enemies. Their fighting ability is exponentially increased. Deuteronomy 32:30 declares that one can chase a thousand, but two can put ten thousand to flight. God's math is different from mankind's. God's 1 plus 1 does not equal 2; it increases exponentially, for according to His math it increases by a power of 10.

During the last four years, the Christian International Apostolic Network staff and the Christian International Vision Church staff have been praying together in tongues for one hour a day. One day God led us in strong warfare in tongues (for our spirit language has the spirit of our mighty warrior God). The Holy Spirit instructed us to expand our application of God's mathematical principle in Deuteronomy 32:30—we no longer limited it to soldiers killing enemies but now regarded it as soldiers producing what we called the Holy Spirit's divine "light power." Jesus declared while on earth, "I am the light of the world" (John 8:12). Then in Matthew 5:14 He declared to His disciples, "You are the light of the world." We have the divine light power of the Christ within us.

Let me give you an example of releasing this kind of power. Most of the time when I lead members of the Church in corporate warfare, I lead them first in a prophetic act of opening heaven above us. According to Deuteronomy 28:1–14, there is nothing more important for your prosperity than having an open heaven. The term *open heaven* is used in verse 12.

Part of our corporate warfare is "against the rulers of the darkness of this age." Jesus declared that light destroys darkness, and darkness cannot withstand the blinding power of divine light. I tell those assembled that we are going to establish an open heaven by pointing up toward one area of the ceiling (or sky, if we are in an open arena). I remind them of when we were in Sunday school and we pointed our forefingers in the air and sang, "This little light of mine, I'm going to let it shine." Then I tell them that we are now going to advance that to an adult warrior level. Habakkuk 3:4 declares that God's rays of light flash from His hand (and finger), and therein is His power revealed. Every one of us has the light of God within.

As a prophetic act of faith, we all point to that one area, believing that God's power will go forth like a light beam. As our thousand Holy Spirit lights come together, they form a gigantic laser beam of Holy Spirit light. As we shout as one, we launch the mighty laser beam to penetrate the power of darkness and make an open portal all the way to the throne of God. I have done this in numerous nations and places and had tremendous results.

All prophetic acts seem foolish to the flesh and nonsensical to the natural mind, whether it is the act of confessing your sins to Jesus and believing that every sin you have ever committed is forgiven, receiving the gift of your Holy Spirit language and praying in a language you have never learned, being healed of leprosy by dipping seven times in the Jordan River, walking around the walls of Jericho and expecting them to fall down when you shout together, or stretching out a rod and expecting the Red Sea to part to the right and left, leaving a dry sea bed for millions of Israelites to walk across. There are too many prophetic acts in Scripture to list. In these days we are praying what Paul told us to pray in Ephesians 1:17–19: for the Spirit of wisdom and revelation, that we might know the exceeding greatness of the power made available to us who believe.

100

Like power produced by electricity, we measure Holy Spirit light power in spiritual "watts." Using Deuteronomy 32:30 as our guide, one saint releasing a shout of faith would produce 1,000 watts of Holy Spirit light power, while one additional saint increases the production to 10,000 watts. Each new addition increases it by another power of 10. As the following chart shows, by the time four of us join together, we have increased production to 1,000,000 watts. Ten saints together produce a *trillion* watts—1 followed by 12 zeros—of Holy Spirit light power. One hundred saints, however, produce an astronomically high level of Holy Spirit light power:

Persons	Watts of Power Produced in the Holy Spirit
1	1,000
2	10,000
3	100,000
4	1,000,000 (million)
5	10,000,000
6	100,000,000
7	1,000,000,000 (billion)
8	10,000,000,000
9	100,000,000,000
10	1,000,000,000,000 (trillion)
13	1,000,000,000,000,000 (quadrillion)
16	1,000,000,000,000,000,000 (quintillion)
100	1 + 303 zeros (centillion)

The joining of the saints in spiritual warfare releases so much power that it is like detonating a weapon of mass destruction. When a hundred unified saints release the shout of faith, it produces more watts of Holy Spirit light power than the Hoover Dam produces watts of electricity in the same length of time. Let's take a closer look at a few of these weapons of mass destruction that do such damage to the enemy.

The Shout of Faith

As I wrote previously, the Church is following the pattern of the Israelites' journey into their Promised Land. The prophetic-apostolic movement of the 1980s and 1990s crossed the Church over its Jordan River. The saints movement in 2007 prepared the way for and activated the third and final Reformation in 2008, which initiated God's World War III. In 2016, by God's decree, the time had come for His army to be activated, going on the offensive to fulfill all of God's prophetic promises to His Church and planet earth.

The Church is now beginning its military conquest. In the restoration process, following God's purpose for the Church, we are now at our Jericho. Like Israel receiving their breakthrough at Jericho with a victorious shout, the Church will begin to gain its breakthroughs by using its most powerful weapon of mass destruction: the *shout of faith*.

In Joshua 6:20, the shout of 600,000 Israelite soldiers caused the tall, thick walls around Jericho to fall down flat. This is a vivid demonstration of the corporate shout of faith. We call it a shout of *faith* because faith is the confident obedience to act upon God's Word. Faith is the victory that overcomes. The shout of faith is the expression of faith, for faith without works is dead, and vocal expression of faith is a work of faith. Though God had commanded Joshua's army to march around the city once a day for six days, on the seventh day He changed His instructions: The army was to start marching by sunrise. The soldiers would march around the city seven times on that final day, and when they finished the seventh circle around the city, the trumpeters would give the signal for all 600,000 soldiers to give a great shout. They were not to say a word before then—but Joshua had seven priests continually blowing their horns during the marching.

Can you imagine the anxiety and fears mounting within the walls of Jericho those seven days? Then they heard the roar of the entire army of Israel shouting—and suddenly their great wall of protection fell to the ground. The next thing—the last thing—they saw was the onslaught of the shouting soldiers flashing their swords as they rushed toward the city from every direction. Within a few hours every resident of the city was dead. The only ones left alive were Rahab and her family, for Joshua had promised to preserve her for hiding the two Israelite spies. The people of Jericho were already in terror before the Israelite army appeared because of the reports of what the God of Israel was doing through them. Listen in on what Rahab told the two spies:

> I know that the LORD has given you the land, that the terror of you has fallen on us, and that all the inhabitants of the land are fainthearted because of you. For we have heard how the LORD dried up the water of the Red Sea for you when you came out of Egypt, and what you did to the two kings of the Amorites who were on the other side of the Jordan, Sihon and Og, whom you utterly destroyed. And as soon as we heard these things, our hearts melted; neither did there remain any more courage in anyone because of you, for the LORD your God, He is God in heaven above and on earth beneath.
>
> Joshua 2:9–11

Rahab's report was a fulfillment of what God had promised Israel: "This day I will begin to put the dread and fear of you upon the nations under the whole heaven, who shall hear the report of you, and shall tremble and be in anguish because of you" (Deuteronomy 2:25).

The Incredible Power of the Shout

This story is significant not only because it portrays the power of the shout of faith, but it is also an illustration of what Christ

Jesus' army, the army of the Lord, will do in the spirit realm against Satan's strongholds and his demonic forces during God's World War III. The Church is entering that phase. The shout of faith is a weapon of mass destruction available to the Church to inflict a tremendous blow on the kingdom of Satan.

We see the power of this weapon in the prophecies of Jesus returning to earth, which He does with a shout:

> For the Lord Himself will descend from heaven with a *shout*, with the voice of an archangel, and with the trumpet of God. And the dead in Christ will rise first. Then we who are alive and remain shall be caught up together with them in the clouds to meet the Lord in the air. And thus we shall always be with the Lord.
>
> 1 Thessalonians 4:16–17

As Jesus returns, He shouts. Why does He shout? Because when Jesus opens His mouth and gives voice to a shout, it releases His resurrection life. That shout is so powerful and creative that it resurrects the bodies of the dead saints and transforms the bodies of the living saints into immortal bodies. It zooms around the world in a flash and resurrects the bodies of every saint who has died over thousands of years. This is the same power that created the heavens and the earth when God opened His mouth and shouted, "Let there be!" and all things that exist came into being.

Most evangelical and Pentecostal ministers call the event described in 1 Thessalonians 4 the Rapture of the Church. Some call it the first resurrection. In it, the saints who have lost their bodies of flesh and bone through death have their bodies restored back to them through resurrection. This makes them whole human beings again, with spirit, soul and body. Then all the saints alive on earth will have their mortal bodies changed into immortal bodies in a moment, in the twinkling of an eye (see 1 Corinthians 15:52; 1 Thessalonians 4:17).

The resurrection of the dead is a major foundational doctrine of Christendom. "If there is no resurrection of the dead," Paul taught, "then Christ is not risen. And if Christ is not risen, then our preaching is empty and your faith is also empty. . . . For if the dead do not rise, then Christ is not risen. And if Christ is not risen, your faith is futile; you are still in your sins!" (1 Corinthians 15:13–14, 16–17). There is no Christianity if there is no resurrection of the dead. Thank God for the resurrecting, translating shout of our Lord and Savior, Jesus Christ.

When we allow the Christ within us to arise in our shout, God assures us that our enemies will be scattered:

Psalm 47:5: "God has gone up with a shout." I view this as a prophetic Scripture about Jesus' return to heaven. I believe it means that when Jesus started ascending to heaven, He gave a shout that launched Him all the way to the throne of God. When we shout, we are to shout with the "voice of triumph" (verse 1).

Numbers 10:35: When Moses, with the Levites carrying the Ark, led the Israelites again on their journey, following the cloud by day and the fire by night, he raised his voice in the hearing of the people and shouted, "Rise up, O LORD! Let Your enemies be scattered, and let those who hate You flee before You."

1 Chronicles 15:28: King David with all Israel brought up the Ark of the Covenant to Jerusalem with shouting.

2 Chronicles 13:15: Judah, with an army of 400,000, was outnumbered and surrounded by an army of 800,000. Judah shouted to God and won the victory, killing 500,000 of their opponents.

Isaiah 42:13: "The LORD shall go forth like a mighty man; He shall stir up His zeal like a man of war. He shall cry out, yes, shout aloud; He shall prevail against His enemies." When God stirs up His zeal to go to battle, He gives a war cry, a loud shout. He knows the shout releases His power like an atomic bomb and activates war angels to join Him in the battle. That is probably the reason God told me that when we give the shout of faith, it explodes in the evil spirit realm like an atomic bomb exploding in the natural realm. It scatters demons in every direction and makes an open heaven over an area.

Numbers 23:19–21: We cannot be cursed when the Lord our God is with us and we allow our shout to go up to God. The King within us will shout through us, causing the glory and power of God to arise and thoroughly scatter our enemies. This was prophesied by the prophet Balaam; he was hired by Balak, king of the Moabites, to curse Israel, for the Moabites felt they needed supernatural help because Israel's God was fighting for them. "Moab was exceedingly afraid of the people [of Israel] because they were many, and Moab was sick with dread because of the children of Israel" (Numbers 22:3). Balaam had a reputation for hundreds of miles that whatever he prophesied would happen. He tried four times in four different places to prophesy judgment and destruction on Israel, but every time he opened his mouth, God made him speak blessings. His second prophecy contains our subject of the shout:

> God is not a man, that He should lie, nor a son of man, that He should repent. Has He said, and will He not do? Or has He spoken, and will He not make it good? Behold, I have received a command to bless; He has blessed, and I cannot reverse it. He has not observed iniquity in Jacob, nor has he seen wickedness in Israel. The LORD his God is with him, and the shout of a King is among them. . . .

There is no sorcery [that will work] against Jacob, nor any divination against Israel.

Numbers 23:19–21, 23

In the New Testament, Jesus, Peter and Jude indicate that Balaam was a false prophet. Nevertheless, God forced him to give true prophecies concerning Israel. The true prophetic word declared that no evil forces, such as witchcraft, occultism or Satanism, can put a curse on us if there is no wickedness or iniquity among us. Let us be assured that if we are walking with God in righteousness, when we shout, God fights for us—so who can withstand us or stop us from achieving God's divine purpose? When we as righteous saints raise up a corporate shout of faith, then God and His holy and mighty war angels join us in our battles to make us more than conquerors.

Psalm 149:6–7, 9: "Let the high praises [shout] of God be in their mouth, and a two-edged sword in their hand, to execute vengeance on the nations. . . . To execute on them the written judgment—this honor have all His saints." Those who are going to serve in God's conquering army must learn how to use their corporate weapon of mass destruction—the shout of faith. In Jeremiah 51:20, the Lord of Hosts says, "You are My battle-ax and weapons of war: For *with you I will break* the nation in pieces; *with you I will destroy* kingdoms [of darkness and evil forces]." Ten times in verses 20–23 God says, "With you I will break/destroy . . ." As I have said, everything God does on earth He does in, with and through His people.

Acts 1:8; Ephesians 3:20: The more of God's power we have within, the more is released when we shout, pray, praise, preach and prophesy. The greatest power producer Jesus gave His Church is the Holy Spirit's gift of a spirit language. The Bible refers to that gift as unknown tongues or speaking in tongues. The charismatics called it receiving the *charism* (gift) of *glossolalia* (tongues). That is why they were called charismatics—just as Pentecostals were called by that name because they preached one could receive the same gift of "unknown tongues" that was given at the birthing of the Church on the day of Pentecost.

One of the best illustrations I use in my book *Seventy Reasons for Speaking in Tongues* (Destiny Image, 2012) is that the gift of a spirit language serves as one's own built-in hydro-electric power plant. The reservoir of water is like being filled with the Spirit, but water in the reservoir is not producing any power, which is one of the major purposes for building a dam. A water gate far below the surface has a turbine in it. When the gate is opened, the rushing water causes the blades of the turbine to spin at a fast pace, which turns the big dynamos that produce electricity. One's water gate is his or her mouth; speaking in tongues is the turbine that activates the spirit-dynamo to produce the powerful presence of God. This is what Jude was referring to when he told the saints to build themselves up in the most holy faith by praying in their spirit languages (see Jude 20). We can create a shout of faith in our spirit languages just as we can in our native tongues. Our spirit languages have the same warrior spirit and nature as Jesus, our mighty warrior.

Prophetic Acts of Faith

What is a prophetic act? It is acting upon a word of instruction from the Bible or a *rhema* word from the Holy Spirit. (*Rhema* refers to the expression of God's thoughts or will through Scripture, through a spoken word from God to an individual, by a word of knowledge or by prophetic revelation). A prophetic act may be following the example of a prophetic act in the Bible. If we act on it in faith, it will produce the results it did in the Bible. Many times the shout was performed as a prophetic act of faith, such as the shout of Joshua and his 600,000 warriors at Jericho. A prophetic act can also be a word of knowledge revealing what to do to produce the results we need. A prophetic act can be revealed through a prophecy that is directed by the Holy Spirit. We will take a look here at some abbreviated illustrations of such acts and the results produced by them.

Jehoshaphat

In 2 Chronicles 20:1–30, we read of King Jehoshaphat of Judah hearing of three great armies, hundreds of thousands of soldiers, that were approaching his nation to destroy them. He became very fearful. There was no way in the natural that Judah could withstand them.

Jehoshaphat called the people together to fast and pray, and God spoke to them through a prophet, saying that they would not need to fight to win this battle:

> Listen, all you of Judah and you inhabitants of Jerusalem, and you, King Jehoshaphat! Thus says the LORD to you: "Do not be afraid nor dismayed because of this great multitude, for the battle is not yours, but God's. Tomorrow go down against them. . . . You will not need to fight in this battle. Position yourselves, stand still and see the salvation of the LORD, who is with you, O Judah and Jerusalem!" Do not fear or be dismayed; tomorrow go out against them, for the LORD is with you.
>
> 2 Chronicles 20:15–17

Once again, God was going to fight for His people. Jehoshaphat received a word of knowledge concerning what to do to cooperate with God in fulfilling the prophecy. He went against all the rules in his war manual. He put the singers and worshipers out in front of the ones equipped with shields and swords. Jehoshaphat encouraged and challenged his people to "believe in the LORD your God, and you shall be established; believe His prophets, and you shall prosper" (verse 20). They knew Psalm 22:3, which declares that God is enthroned in [inhabits] the praises of His people. So they stood to "praise the LORD God of Israel with voices loud and high" (verse 19).

When they did this prophetic act, God fought their battle for them. He sent His war angels to turn the invading armies against each other, so that they killed one another until every soldier was dead:

> So when Judah came to a place overlooking the wilderness, they looked toward the multitude; and there were their dead bodies, fallen on the earth. No one had escaped. When Jehoshaphat and his people came to take away their spoil, they found among them an abundance of valuables on the dead bodies, and precious jewelry, which they stripped off for themselves, more than they could carry away; and they were three days gathering the spoil because there was so much.
>
> 2 Chronicles 20:24–25

What a triumphant victory from one prophetic act of faith!

Moses

In Exodus 14, Moses did a prophetic act in obedience to the command of the Lord. He stretched his rod out toward the Red Sea, and it rolled back, allowing God's people to escape safely across. When the Egyptians entered the waters, divided and walled up on either side, with their army of 600 chariots, 200,000 footmen and many horsemen, God told Moses to again stretch his rod out over the waters—another prophetic act. When he did, all of Pharaoh's army drowned, leaving God's people free to continue on toward their Promised Land.

God nearly always has His saints do something that demonstrates their obedience and faith in God's word, whether that word is in the Bible or spoken prophetically or is a *rhema* word of knowledge. It probably has something to do with the Scripture that says that faith without works is *dead*. There can be actions that are not acted out in faith, but there can be no demonstration of biblical faith without corresponding action, verbally or physically (see James 2:14–26). True prophetic acts are faith in action. Dead faith does not take action, but living faith always takes action.

When Moses and the children of Israel were traveling through the wilderness, the Amalekites attacked them. Joshua led the men in battle against them (see Exodus 17:8–16). Moses did a prophetic act and held up his hands for victory. When his hands were up, Joshua was winning; when his hands lowered, the enemy began winning. Aaron and Hur saw what was happening and got on each side of Moses to hold his hands up until Joshua won the battle. There is no logical reason that Moses keeping his hands above his head would help Joshua win the battle except for God honoring the prophetic faith act of Moses.

Jacob

Jacob worked twenty years for his uncle Laban to secure his wife Rachel. During that time, Laban changed Jacob's wages ten times. In one discussion of payment, Jacob made a deal with Laban that he would take all the sheep that were born with mixed colors; Laban would take all of the solid-colored sheep. Most of the sheep were solid colored, leaving Jacob very little chance to increase his number of sheep, for a solid-colored sheep bred to a solid-colored buck would continue to have solid-colored lambs. So Jacob did a prophetic act—one so improbable and impossible that I am going to quote the account of it directly from the Bible:

> Then Jacob took rods of fresh-cut poplar, almond, and plane trees, and peeled white streaks in them, exposing the white which was in the rods. He set the rods which he had peeled before the flocks in the troughs, that is, the watering places, where the flocks came to drink, so that they would mate when they came to drink. The flocks mated before the rods and gave birth to young that were striped, speckled, and spotted. Jacob separated the lambs and made the flocks face toward the striped and all the brown in the flock of Laban. He put his own flocks by themselves and did not put them with Laban's sheep. Whenever the stronger sheep mated, Jacob laid the rods before the eyes of the sheep in the troughs, so that they might mate among the rods. But when the livestock were feeble, he did not put them in. So the weaker were Laban's and the stronger Jacob's. The man [Jacob] became exceedingly prosperous and had many sheep and female servants and male servants and camels and donkeys.
>
> Genesis 30:37–43 MEV

There is no biological explanation why solid-colored sheep looking at a striped and spotted rod should start birthing striped and spotted-colored sheep. Jacob's flock of sheep grew much more numerous than Laban's. There is no scientific or biological explanation, or any logical reason, why Jacob's actions should work—except that Jacob did a prophetic act of faith that God honored. God honors prophetic acts of His people when they dare to believe that if they can conceive it, they can achieve it. And God will work with them to make it work when it is not supposed to work according to the laws of nature. There is more to the Scripture "With God all things are possible" than we have comprehended.

Other Biblical Acts of Faith

Most prophetic acts are illogical; they do not make sense, and it seems foolish to the natural-minded saint to act them out. For instance, the prophet Elisha told Captain Naaman of Syria to do a prophetic act of dipping seven times in the Jordan River to be healed of his leprosy. He thought it sounded ridiculous. He refused at first, but when he relented and did what Elisha said, he was healed of his leprosy.

Elisha did a prophetic act of throwing a stick in the river where an iron ax head had fallen; the ax head floated to the top and swam to shore. Another time he told a widow to do a prophetic act of gathering all the vessels she could borrow and then use her single pint of oil to fill all of them. Logic and reason said that could never work, but she did her prophetic act of faith, and her pint of oil filled gallons and barrels with oil. She paid off her bills, bought several things she needed and probably put her boys through college with the money she made by selling that oil over the next several years.

Modern Prophetic Acts of Faith

There are many more examples of prophetic acts of faith in the Bible, but the ones we have covered should be sufficient to convince you that prophetic acts are a biblical principle and that they produce miraculous results. Now I want to share with you some present-day prophetic acts that accomplished great things for God, His Church and special people for whom the prophetic acts were performed.

The Pacific Rim

In 1992 two different prophets, at two different times and places, prophesied that I was to go to the Pacific Rim nations

113

and war against Satan's plans. I sought the Lord for several weeks to determine what the Lord was trying to convey to me. He finally brought vision and revelation that Satan was seeking to start World War III between the East and the West and that he would try to start this war between 1992 and 2001. Christ revealed that China (a major Communist nation), an Islamic nation and Russia were making secret negotiations to conquer the world and divide it among themselves. These secret communications were like the trilateral agreement that Germany, Japan and Italy made at the beginning of World War II.

God spoke to me personally, confirming that I was to go to the Pacific Rim nations. In the natural I did not know what those nations were or where they were located in the world. After researching world maps, I discovered that the Pacific Rim nations are simply those whose coasts touch the Pacific Ocean. The Lord said that if I would go and lead the ministers of many of these nations in spiritual warfare with the shout of faith, we could stop the war plans of Satan—but it would take several battles over several years to win the war. He said if we only partially fought, we would win a percentage in the Spirit but the rest would have to be fought with natural soldiers and world weapons. But if we fought all the way to defeating the evil plans, there would be no "Satan's World War III" started at this time.

My wife and I, with teams of saints and ministers, started going to the Pacific Rim nations that God showed us and doing spiritual warfare. We went to some of these countries several times between 1992 and 2001. Most often we traveled to South Korea, Japan, Philippines, Malaysia, Indonesia, Singapore, Taiwan, Hong Kong, Australia, New Zealand and California and Alaska in America. We went to Singapore the most because it seemed to be the best place to do spiritual warfare. I will use our efforts in Singapore as an example of what we did in each nation.

While we were there, I taught on what I have shared with you in this chapter. I had all the ministers attending join me on the stage (there were around a hundred). We invited all the musicians to use their instruments to do warfare with those who do the shouting. They were instructed not to play a chorus with rhythm but to play in the same key and give me all the volume they could, especially with the drums. I then explained to the ministers that we were all going to point toward China and shout against Satan's plans to start World War III. All the ministers on the platform and the congregation believed the prophet and acted upon the word of God; they shouted aloud with great enthusiasm for 45 minutes. Several of the ministers and some of the saints had visions and saw into the spirit realm. People saw something like rockets being launched and hitting areas occupied by evil principalities and satanic agents who were influencing China and the other nations involved. Others saw the archangel Michael and his war angels leading divisions of angels in different directions to fulfill the purpose of our war-cry shout of faith. This took place in every nation where we did corporate spiritual warfare. In the spring of 2001 God spoke again, saying that we had caused confusion in the enemy's effort for a trilateral agreement and had completely defeated the plans of Satan to start an East-West World War III.

Because Satan was stopped from starting a war between the nations, he changed his tactic to a war of terrorism. In America it was launched on September 11, 2001, the day the Twin Towers of the World Trade Center in New York were destroyed when terrorists flew jetliners into them, causing them to crumble to the ground. We are to this day in a war unlike any world wars that came before. For terrorism to be defeated will require the army of the Lord to arise and fight against and destroy the rulers of darkness, evil principalities and powers that are inspiring and empowering the terrorists. The armies of the nations and intelligence agents in the natural will do all they can to defeat them. God knows, however, that the battles must first be won in the spirit realm before they can be won in the natural.

Bogotá, Colombia

A few years back I was with Pastor Ricardo Rodriguez and his church in Colombia. He had twenty thousand attending the 8:30 service and twenty thousand attending the 10:30. The Lord revealed to me that there was a drug lord the police and military had been trying to catch for ten years. Every time they would get close to capturing him, satanic forces of witchcraft and other spirit beings would warn him, and he would always escape. I told the people that I was going to lead them in spiritual warfare, and we were going to remove all of his covering and assistance in the spirit realm. I taught them on the Church's most powerful corporate weapon of warfare, the shout of faith. I then led them in using the shout of the saints as a weapon of mass destruction against the enemy. Those who know how to allow the Christ within them to arise in the shout will scatter their enemies. They were a believing and enthusiastic church; they shouted with faith and zeal of the Lord for thirty minutes. Two days later the headlines in the newspaper read that the drug lord they had been trying to capture had been captured. He is still in jail today.

When we direct our shout at a particular situation, war angels are released and sent to do whatever is necessary to fulfill the purpose of the shout. They war in the spirit realm while we war with our prophetic acts of faith. Remember, according to God's math, one warrior saint can produce 1000 watts of Holy Spirit light power, while four saints can produce one million, seven can produce one billion, ten can produce one trillion, and a hundred can produce 1 + 303 zeros. It is beyond imagination to grasp how many watts of divine light power those twenty thousand shouting saints were producing.

Akwa Ibom, Nigeria, Africa

In September 2016 I was in Nigeria to do a four-day conference on prophets and corporate spiritual warfare. The conference was hosted by Archbishop Cletus Bassey of Destiny International Missions and a network of prophetic ministers, and it was approved by His Excellency Udom Emmanuel, governor of Akwa Ibom state. Apostle Leon Walters and Pastor Enos Chamberlain accompanied me. They did the teaching and workshops during the day, and I did the preaching at night. On Wednesday night I taught on prophetic acts, activating the people in the prophetic at the end. Thursday night I preached on Jesus the mighty warrior and led them in establishing an open heaven over their area. On Friday night I preached on corporate warfare as the army of the Lord. We directed our warfare at the Islamic force trying to infiltrate south Nigeria. We were also warring for the birthing of the third Church Reformation in Nigeria. In many nations and places where we have done warfare, there have been confirming signs such as angels, wind, fire, hailstorms and many saints having visions of what is taking place in the spirit realm. This time the sign was different. A young lady had a baby right there at the church, while three thousand saints were warring with their shout of faith. The next night they brought the baby and had me hold her up in dedication and as a sign of the new Nigeria that had just been birthed into the Third Reformation.

The governor of the state, who is a Christian, had us stay in a nice home on the governor's compound. He insisted we stay with him so that we would have diplomatic immunity. We had armed guards and military vehicles to take us wherever we went. On Monday before we left, the governor called a special session of his cabinet so that I could speak to them and give the word of the Lord for their state and nation. They presented me with a plaque at the meeting, saying it is the highest honor that they can bestow upon a person. We prophesied to the former and present governor. They declared they believed God had caused a shift in the nation. We are expecting God to begin doing even greater things in Nigeria.

Mexico City, Mexico

About three thousand saints gathered for a conference where I taught on spiritual corporate warfare with the shout of faith. I also used many Scriptures to prove that God personally fights for us when we go to war against our enemies that are also God's enemies. To portray to them that God personally fights with His own hands to kill human enemies, I used the story of Joshua defeating the Amorite kings in Joshua 10, which I described in detail in chapter 5. This was the time that God used His hailstone bombs to win the victory for the Israelites and supernaturally extended the day so that the Israelites would have more time to defeat their enemies. God likewise used hailstone bombs to implement some of His judgments on Egypt (see Exodus 9:18–26), and He will use hailstone bombs again to execute His judgment in the destruction of Babylon (see Revelation 16:19–21).

After teaching on Jesus the mighty warrior, who uses hailstones as weapons, I led them in the shout of faith. About ten minutes into the shout, there came a tremendous noise inside that tin-roofed building. Some young people ran outside to see what was happening. They came back in with handfuls of hailstones about the size of golf balls. It was a hail storm in the middle of July in Mexico City. I exhorted the people that this was confirmation that God was going to fight for the Mexican Christians. Joshua proclaimed in his day of battle that "the LORD fought for Israel." They will likewise be able to say of the day we did spiritual warfare through our prophetic act of shouting that the Lord fought for Mexico.

Papua New Guinea

The directors of the Christian International Global Network, Prophet Jim Stevens and Apostle Judy Stevens, were the first to go to Papua New Guinea on behalf of Christian International. An apostle in Papua New Guinea by the name of Dion Warep wanted to come under the covering of the prophetic and apostolic with the Kingdom of God, which Christian International was pioneering and establishing throughout the world. I went the next year with Jim and Judy and preached on the Third Reformation, with emphasis on the Kingdom of God. On the last night I led them in corporate warfare. We warred against corruption in the government. The next day a warrant was issued for the president to be arrested for corruption in the government. The next year when I came, they prepared a luncheon at the capital in my honor, at which the Speaker of the House and I spoke. He enumerated many good things that had happened in the country since we started coming to their nation and doing spiritual warfare.

For the first time in the history of the nation, all the different church denominations were attending the conference, along with police, military and government officials. I figured I should preach messages that all could receive without offending anyone. But on the last night, to my surprise, God told me to preach on spiritual warfare for the transformation of the nation in righteousness and decreasing violence, so that Papua New Guinea would become a Kingdom nation practicing the principles of the Kingdom and demonstrating its power. I taught them about the shout of faith being the spiritual weapon that goes off in the spiritual realm the way an atomic bomb does in the natural. We brought the musicians to the platform to do warfare with their instruments while the congregation shouted. Some of the military, police and government officials were not Christians, and the denominational preachers and saints had never done anything like this. I wondered how they would respond. But, praise God, to my amazement, everyone in that stadium lifted hands and shouted enthusiastically for fifteen minutes. I discovered that people who love their nations are willing to do things they do not fully understand and are not accustomed to doing if they are convinced it will benefit the nation, which ends up benefiting them. One pastor asked a non-Christian policeman why he shouted. He replied, "The preacher said it would reduce the crime rate, and I want to do anything that will reduce the violence and crime in our nation."

Again, let us remember that the destination of a nation is determined by God's word to that nation. God's prophets speak God's words, and the Church enforces that prophetic word through prophetic warfare, intercession and becoming involved in leadership, gaining decision-making positions in the nation. Some are called to judge and execute God's judgments through spiritual warfare; others are called to be kingdom influencers in the seven mountains of culture (see Revelation 2:26–27; 5:10; 11:15; 21:24; Matthew 25:31, 34, 41; 1 Corinthians 6:2–3; Psalm 149:5–9). If we really believe we are going to rule and reign with Christ on the new earth over the sheep nations during the millennial reign, then it would be good to get some on-the-job training now.

ENLIGHTENMENT, DECLARATION AND PRAYER

Lord Jesus, I accept Your Word that Christians have weapons of warfare and we are to use them to pull down evil strongholds and destroy the works of Satan. I am called to resist the devil and do personal spiritual warfare, but You also have a purpose for corporate warfare by the Church. The more saints who join in the shout of faith, the more Holy Spirit light power is produced to destroy whole armies of evil forces, like a weapon of mass destruction. Lord, I will be a warrior in Your army and participate in the Church's corporate warfare of destroying the works of the devil: "For this purpose the Son of God was manifested, that He might destroy the works of the devil" (1 John 3:8). "As the Father has sent Me, I also send you" (John 20:21).

8

Can the Few Affect the Many?

There is a commonly accepted saying in Christendom that "prayer changes things." To explain how and why prayer changes things could require a whole book in itself. The fact is that God has given ways to mankind for us to impact the world. Anything Satan has planned or any works that he is doing can be changed or negated by the army of the Lord when they take up their weapons. Anything contrary to God's Word, will and way can be changed. The Church is God's delegated authority on earth to fulfill God's prophetic purposes. During God's World War III, revelation and faith will be given to the army of the Lord to do things that will cause transformation of nations.

We must receive divine revelation from God concerning what works of the enemy we are authorized to go against and destroy. An individual, for example, should not try to take on an enemy that requires the power of corporate warfare. But corporately, even when we are small in numbers, we have exponential power to change the atmospheres of cities and nations. Remember that the power produced by each new warrior increases by a power of 10. One can produce 1000 watts of Holy Spirit light power, two can produce 10,000, sixteen can produce a quintillion and a hundred warriors can produce unlimited power—1 + 303 zeros. Jesus declared that He gave us all authority over all the power of the enemy (see Luke 10:19). Through His death on the cross and resurrection from the dead, Jesus took all power from the devil and gave all power to His Church. He commissioned His Church as the corporate Body of Christ. Jesus has done and accomplished everything He was supposed to do in His personal body. It is now His greatest pleasure and purpose to finish fulfilling prophetic Scriptures through His corporate body until the time comes for Him to fulfill the prophetic Scripture of His return in His glorified earth body.

What Can One Man Do?

The Word of God declares that it makes no difference to the Lord to save by many or by a few (see 1 Samuel 14:6). You may wonder if it is possible for a few Christian warriors to do spiritual warfare that can affect national affairs. Yes, they can! Mankind's God-given authority gives even an individual tremendous power to affect the world. One man's action of disobedience to God caused all mankind to become sinners. That one man's sin destined every human to die, for through Adam's offense, judgment came to all men, resulting in condemnation and death (see Romans 5:12–19). One man, Christ Jesus, gave His life on the cross of Calvary and made redemption available for the whole human race. By one man's sacrifice you and I were redeemed, given eternal life and made members of the corporate Body of Christ. One young man by the name of David stood against a great giant who was defying the whole army of Israel; with a simple weapon, his slingshot, David gave the soldiers of Israel the victory that day. One man's act of warfare affected King Saul's army and the whole nation of Israel.

Now is our time and opportunity to give our lives in service to Jesus Christ and to help Him build His corporate Body, the Church, to the number of members God desires to make the Body of Christ complete (see Revelation 6:11), attaining to the ministry and maturity God has purposed. We can also be His warriors, co-laboring with Him in His ministry of destroying the works of the devil. One of the major ways we can do this is with our devil-destroying weapon of mass destruction—the corporate shout of faith.

During the run-up to the Iraq War, which began in March 2003, the U.S. military prepared for thousands of American soldiers to die in the initial invasion of Iraq. They sent numerous body bags to the area with that expectation. At Christian International's annual October conference in 2002, the International Gathering of Apostles and Prophets, God spoke to us that the devil had plans to kill sixty thousand soldiers from America and her allies. Jesus said He wanted us to go into spiritual warfare and stop the plans of Satan in order to save fifty thousand of them. On a Wednesday evening, we did this for thirty minutes, targeting Satan's plans. We decreed and shouted until we felt assurance that the battle was won. I wondered why God had told us to fight for only fifty thousand out of the sixty thousand.

Three weeks later I was in Tulsa, Oklahoma, and shared this with the church I was preaching at. The pastor grew excited and asked the exact time of our warfare. When I told him, he explained that on that very same Wednesday night, God had spoken to them to do the very same thing—except that He told them to do spiritual warfare for ten thousand. God had our conference of a thousand saints do spiritual warfare to save the fifty thousand, and He had the church of two hundred saints save the ten thousand.

Not long after, the U.S. forces invaded Iraq. Several media outlets reported that just before they did, the military leadership changed their plans for the location of the invasion. They announced that if they had not changed their plans, tens of thousands would have been killed; in fact, very few died in the battle.

What Changes When Saints Fight?

Jesus has an army of angels in heaven and an army of warrior saints on earth. He has authorized them to work together to accomplish His purpose until God's Kingdom comes and His will is done on earth as it is in heaven. Jesus' war angels fight in the heavenlies while His Church fights on earth with prophetic acts of faith. War angels are real, and they are commissioned by almighty God to assist us who are working to fulfill God's purposes for His Church and planet earth.* Many examples of this principle are demonstrated in the Bible.

David: Changing the City and Nation

When King David prepared to make war with the Philistines (see 2 Samuel 5:22–25), he was told by the Lord to wait. I believe he had to wait until Michael and his war angels launched their attack in the spirit realm before David could launch his attack with his army. God said David would know the time of the beginning of the battle when the tops of the trees began bending toward the battle, as the war angels launched their attack. At that moment, David was to launch his attack against the Philistines in coordination with the angels. The angel armies in heaven worked with David's army on earth to destroy the Philistine army.

Jonathan: One Man with a Plan

One man and His armor bearer did an act of warfare that delivered and transformed a whole nation. I wrote about this

---

* A good friend of mine, Pastor Tim Sheets, wrote a book—with a foreword from his brother, Dutch Sheets—called *Angel Armies* (Destiny Image, 2016), in which he presents all the activities and ministries of angels.

event in chapter 3. The Philistines had set up garrisons throughout the land in order to rule Israel. Jonathan, son of King Saul, attacked one of those garrisons, provoking the Philistines to such anger that they brought up their whole army to annihilate Israel. Israel was overwhelmingly outnumbered. Jonathan decided to try the ridiculous: He and his armor bearer would expose themselves to the warriors in the Philistine garrison. If they invited the two to come up the hill and enter the garrison, it would be a sign that God was going to give Jonathan and his armor bearer the victory, though they were only two against hundreds in the camp. It was Jonathan who declared that "nothing restrains the LORD from saving by many or by few" (1 Samuel 14:6). Two will do if God and His holy war angels join us in the battle.

The Philistines challenged them to come up; they did and dispatched twenty soldiers of their own. Then God started shaking the earth and the war angels swept in, bringing fear and confusion upon the Philistines. As a result, the enemy fled and Israel was delivered from the rule and oppression of the Philistines. One man and his assistant affected a whole nation with just a little daring warfare, powerfully motivating heaven to join the battle.

Gideon: Never Too Few, Sometimes Too Many

God has never told His people that they did not have enough resources or people to win a battle, but He did tell Gideon that he had too many. God announced to Gideon that He was going to use him to deliver Israel from the great horde of Midianites who were invading their land (see Judges 7). Gideon blew the war trumpet to summon the warriors to fight, and 32,000 showed up. Gideon no doubt asked the Lord if 32,000 was enough to go against more than 300,000. God responded that it was the opposite—Gideon had too many.

So God had Gideon tell everyone who was afraid to go home, and 22,000 left. Gideon's next question would have been, "Is the remaining 10,000 enough?" Nope—still too many. Gideon took them to the river and tested them there, and only three hundred passed the test. I think God must have said something to the effect of, "Now the odds are just right." For He knew His own divine decree, that one Israelite would be able to chase a thousand of their enemies. He had promised them that, as the Lord their God, He would fight for them: "One man of you shall chase a thousand, for the LORD your God is He who fights for you, as He promised you" (Joshua 23:10). By that formula, the number of fighters with Gideon was the right one: three hundred Israelites could put 300,000 Midianites to flight.

Gideon and the three hundred blew their trumpets at midnight and shouted. God sent confusion, fear and terror into the enemy's camp. The war angels swept down among them, scattering them in every direction. That day less than one tenth of 1 percent of the population of Israel brought freedom and economic prosperity to the whole nation. A few warrior saints doing spiritual warfare with the shout of faith bring transformation to a city, state or nation. The few can affect the many! This truth needs to be born within every Christian warrior.

Esther: Right Place at the Right Time

A young Jewish girl, Esther, was chosen to be queen to King Ahasuerus of Persia, a ruler so powerful that he controlled 127 provinces from India to Ethiopia. The Jews had been brought to Persia as captives and were scattered throughout the provinces. A right-hand man of the king developed a hatred for them and talked the king into passing a decree: On a certain date, the people could kill anyone who was a Jew and take all that person's possessions. The king agreed to this without knowing that Esther herself was a Jew. Mordecai, her cousin and former guardian, sent word to Esther that she must intercede to save her people, for she was at the right place in the right position at the proper time.

Esther objected. "If I go," she sent word to Mordecai, "I could be executed. No one may go before the king without being invited. If I go and the king does not extend his scepter to me, it will be the end of my life." In the end, however, she decided she would do it; if she perished, then she perished, but she was trusting God to give her favor with the king. Esther prayed and fasted until she had the faith and courage to put her life on the line for the sake of her people. She received that favor and revealed to the king the wicked plan against her people. She obtained a decree from the king that the Jews could fight back. They destroyed all those who tried to destroy them. One girl saved God's people from annihilation. Can one person make a difference if that person is willing to lay down his or her life for the cause of Christ Jesus and His people? Yes!

What We Can and Cannot Change

There are several types of praying, but the one most people think of is asking God for needs to be met—asking help for oneself and petitioning on behalf of others. One of the main reasons this works—that prayer can change people and situations—is because God established a law of prayer. Jesus told His followers that if we ask, we shall receive; if we seek, we shall find; if we knock, the door shall be opened to us. And if we ask anything in Jesus' name, He will do it (see Matthew 7:7; John 14:13–14). The Word of God says we have not because we ask not. This does not mean praying to just anyone or anything, but only praying to our heavenly Father in the name of Jesus Christ our Lord.

Now that we know the basic reason why we are to pray, let us look at *how* prayer changes things. How can our praying cause someone else to be saved or healed? How can it bring about change in others' behavior? For God follows His own law of free will for mankind. He will not force anyone to do anything against that person's will. So how can praying for someone to be saved help? It is like the way an airplane flies. The airplane does not break the law of gravity when it takes off and remains in the air. It is merely following the laws of aerodynamics. The laws of aerodynamics do not do away with the law of gravity; they just supersede it for a time. God does not do away with man's free will, either; He just supersedes it until man finally chooses God's will. He does not make us go against our will, He just makes us willing to go. Prayer for unsaved loved ones gives God the legal right to do whatever is necessary to make the person willing to choose to serve God.

Heaven does nothing on earth unless someone has prayed about it first. For every person who is saved, someone prayed for him or her first. Someone that knew that lost person prayed for salvation, or the Holy Spirit directed someone using a spirit language to pray for that person in an unknown tongue. Regardless of whether we understand the whys and hows of a biblical truth, principle or practice, we should act upon it, believing that it will produce the results God promised. I do not fully understand when I eat beef, pork or chicken how I do not turn into them but they become me. I do not understand how different-colored vegetables that I consume turn into my skin color. If my African-American brother eats the same vegetables, they turn into his color. I do not worry about understanding the details of how it works; I just sit down at the table and enjoy eating meat and vegetables. Most people do not understand the workings of many things they use and benefit from every day, such as cell phones, cars, televisions, computers and the internet. We can likewise benefit from prayer without understanding its ins and outs; we just have to do it.

That is the main reason Scripture says we should not lean on our own understanding but rather trust in the Lord (see Proverbs 3:5). If it is a biblical principle, for example Psalm 34:3–8, then keep believing and practicing it until it accomplishes God's purpose for Himself and fulfillment in your life.

As basic and essential as prayer is, it is only the first step in producing the results needed and in fulfilling God's purpose. In most stories of great accomplishment in the Bible, the people follow the same steps: They cry out to God in prayer. God sends a prophet to give words of correction, adjustment and encouragement. Then God raises up a deliverer with a plan and God-given power and wisdom to fulfill it. The chosen deliverer takes personal action or raises up an army to meet the needs of the people and fulfill God's timely purpose.

This process of deliverance, transformation and prophetic fulfillment is exemplified in Israel crying out to God in their bondage in Egypt. God sent the prophet Moses to deliver them and then anointed Joshua head of the Israelite army to possess the Promised Land. Praying got them out, God's miraculous workings brought them on their journey to the Jordan River, and it was warfare by Joshua's army that enabled them to possess Canaan.

Judges 6 recounts how God's people had been oppressed and robbed of their crops and cattle for seven years by the Midianites. Finally, after seven years of this oppression, they cried out to God, who sent a prophet to remind them that He worked miracles to bring their forefathers out of Egypt (see verses 8–10). He helped the Joshua generation destroy the Amorites who occupied the land. He reminded them of God's commands to not serve the gods of the Amorites or to fear them. Then he prophesied that they had not obeyed the voice of the Lord.

But now, because they were His people and had cried out to Him, turning from their wicked ways, He would fulfill the promise He would later make to Solomon after the dedication of the Temple: "If My people who are called by My name will humble themselves, and pray and seek my face, and turn from their wicked ways, then I will hear from heaven, and will forgive their sin and heal their land" (2 Chronicles 7:12). Prayer and repentance activated the process. The prophet moved it to the next phase of fulfillment. God then raised up a deliverer, Gideon, who brought forth an elite special force of warriors whose warfare destroyed the enemy and drove them out, enabling the Israelites' land to be healed. The courageous and faithful few obtained the breakthrough; then the other tribes joined them in bringing deliverance, transformation and prosperity to the whole nation. The entire process started out with prayer but finished with warfare.

We are now at the finishing of the age of the mortal Church. Prayer is foundational and essential for every generation, but now spiritual warfare must be added. God is bringing forth His special force of courageous Joshua-generation warriors who will fight until every prophetic Scripture is fulfilled and God's purpose for His mortal Church here on earth is accomplished.

Unconditional Prophecies

In my book *Prophets and Personal Prophecy* (Destiny Image, 2001), I present the ideas of conditional prophecies and unconditional prophecies. Unconditional prophecies are divine decrees that God has made that cannot be altered or stopped, for they are dependent only on God's ability to make sure they come to pass. An example of this kind of prophecy is Daniel's interpretation of the dream of Nebuchadnezzar, king of Babylon. He saw in his dream a great statue with a head of gold, chest of silver, loins of bronze and feet of iron and clay. Daniel's interpretation revealed that the head of gold represented Nebuchadnezzar's present kingdom, while the silver, bronze and iron-clay represented three successive kingdoms. History reveals that those four kingdoms were Babylon, Medo-Persia, Greece and Rome. The rise of these kingdoms was not dependent on God's people praying or the obedience of any person but strictly God directing the affairs of men.

Daniel prophesied that during the fourth kingdom a stone would be cut out of a mountain without human hands, and that stone would establish a kingdom that would end up destroying all the other kingdoms, growing into a great mountain that would fill the whole earth and last forever. This refers to Jesus the Rock and His Church Kingdom. As surely as the four kingdoms in history were real and fulfilled Daniel's prophecy, so will Jesus and His Church destroy all the wicked off the earth and establish a new earth where only righteousness will dwell and rule. Satan and all of his evil forces cannot stop this from happening. No human being can stop it or keep it from coming to pass in God's timing and purpose (see Daniel 2:34–45; Isaiah 2:2; 2 Peter 3:13; Revelation 5:10; Matthew 6:10).

Conditional, Partial and Progressive Prophecies

Unconditional prophecies are general prophecies; personal prophecies, on the other hand, are not unconditional. Rather they operate on three principles: They are conditional, partial and progressive. All personal prophecies can be altered, postponed, partially fulfilled, completely fulfilled or never fulfilled. There are more examples of personal prophecies in the Bible than any kind of prophecy.

Directive words from the Lord, such as God's instruction to Moses about building the Tabernacle or to Noah about building the Ark, are personal prophecies. So are all prophecies giving personal direction to individuals or even nations. They were given to a certain person at a particular time for a special purpose and are not to be repeated by someone else; thus they are conditional on the circumstances in which God gave them. A person cannot open the Bible, say, *Lord, speak to me through whatever Scripture my finger touches*, and assume that God is telling him to do whatever is in that Scripture. If his finger falls on the Scripture of God telling Noah to build the Ark, he cannot assume that God is telling him to literally build an ark. Most of the things God told people to do in the Old Testament came through personal prophecies; Moses, Noah, Solomon and many of the prophets received this kind of word. For instance, God told Isaiah to walk naked through the streets of Israel for three years to portray the nakedness of Israel before God. Though it is Scripture, it is a personal prophecy that only applied to Isaiah in his day.

A personal prophecy is partial in that it will not reveal the whole life and ministry of a person. Abraham received eleven personal prophecies in his lifetime. Each one revealed more details of his life and ministry. I have experienced the same in my life; I received my first personal prophecy from a prophet in 1952. I started giving personal prophecies a year later. When I used to prophesy over hundreds of people in one setting, at the end of our meetings, some of the ministers and saints would pray for me and speak personal prophecies. I have several three- and five-inch binders full of personal prophecies received over the years—2,500 pages of them! I can honestly say that out of all of those prophecies I received, from new converts to mature prophets, less than 1 percent were not of God, which means that 99 percent were scriptural and in line with God's call and destiny for my life.

It took several descendant generations to fulfill all of Abraham's personal prophecies. This is an example of how personal prophecies are progressive. I am glad personal prophecies are generational and that my children, grandchildren and great-grandchildren will be fulfilling them until Jesus comes. The conditional, partial and progressive nature of personal prophecies applies to prophecies of blessings and to prophecies of judgment, such as the one given by the prophet Jonah to Nineveh.

Be assured that no devil in hell or man on earth can keep you from fulfilling all your personal prophecies; only you can do that, for personal prophecy is fulfilled on the condition of your submission and complete obedience to God's personal directives. Only the overcomers receive the reward of ruling and reigning, for they are the called, chosen and faithful. Let us faithfully fulfill all that God has commissioned us to be and do so that we can hear those eternally important words, "Well done, good and faithful servant!"

ENLIGHTENMENT, DECLARATION AND PRAYER

Father God, I sometimes feel insignificant and wonder if I as an individual can make a difference. But the truths and illustrations in this chapter prove that one person can make a difference. Jesus, give me the faith and willingness to put my life on the line just as David, Jonathan and Esther did to bring great deliverance to Your people. I want to be one of the overcomers from Revelation 12:11: "And they did not love their lives to the death." I receive Your grace and boldness to do all You have called me to do for You and with You. Amen.

9

The Army of the Lord

God has even more in mind for His Church than for them to stand in the gap as intercessors for their nations. He wants nothing less than to establish the fullness of God's Kingdom here on earth, as it already is in heaven. For this He needs an army. God has been preparing His Church to become an invincible, unstoppable, unconquerable, overcoming army capable of subduing everything under Christ's feet (see Hebrews 10:13). God is sovereignly moving to restore all that is needed for Christ's army to be and do what God has eternally purposed. The generals who will lead this army will be those who have progressively been prepared by incorporating every restoration truth into their lives and ministries. When all is ready, He will activate the army of the Lord movement. This process has already begun.

> Who is she [Bride of Christ] that looketh forth as the morning, fair as the moon, clear as the sun, and terrible [awesome] as an army with banners? . . . Return, return, O Shulamite [Church]; return, return [repent, be prepared and fully restored], that we

may look upon thee. What will ye see in the Shulamite [fully restored Church]? As it were the *company of two armies.*

Song of Songs 6:10, 13 KJV

The Bride of Christ Is a Warrior

Jesus' great end time army is being prepared to execute God's written judgments through Christ's victory and through divine decrees of judgment that have already been established in heaven. The time is set when these decrees will be executed on earth through God's saintly army. As the Church, we are to be the fulfillment of God's prophecy to Abraham that his seed would bless the whole earth. All that is destined and needed to fulfill this purpose is being activated through God's movement to restore the army of the Lord.

In fact, the Church has always been God's army. But historically it has both lain dormant and been called to action during "cold" wars and "hot" wars. During the Dark Ages it was defeated and disbanded. Nevertheless, the Church was reactivated into a militant spiritual army in 1517, at the beginning of the Second Reformation, which began the great restoration of the Church (see Acts 3:21).

Since the days of Martin Luther, God has raised up spiritual generals every hundred years or so to lead the Church in restoring another truth (see Table 1). Martin Luther was general in his day, leading the Church in many battles until they had fully restored and established the truths of the Protestant movement. Other generals were raised up in cyclical fashion to fulfill God's purposes in the Church, up until 1950. At that point, the battles to restore truth began to take place roughly every ten years. Now we have crossed the Jordan and entered a war for the Church's Promised Land—earth. This war will not cease until all the enemies of God are destroyed and Christ

Table 1. Restoration of Truth Ministries and Founding of Individual Movements/Denominations in the Second Reformation of the Church

Approximate Year	Movement	Major Truths Restored	Denominations Founded
1500	Protestant	Salvation by grace through faith (Ephesians 2:8–9).	Lutheran, Episcopalian, Presbyterian, Congregational
1600	Evangelical	Water baptism, rejection of a national Church.	Mennonite, Baptist, all evangelical churches
1700	Holiness	Sanctification, setting apart of the Church from the world.	Methodist, Nazarene, Church of God, all Holiness churches
1800	Faith Healing	Divine physical healing in the atonement.	Christian and Missionary Alliance, Church of God
1900	Pentecostal	Holy Spirit baptism with unknown tongues.	Assemblies of God, Foursquare, Church of God in Christ
1950	Latter Rain	Prophetic presbytery, singing praises, Body of Christ membership ministries.	Nondenominational churches
1950	Deliverance Evangelism	*Evangelist* ministry, mass evangelism reactivated with miraculous healings.	Independent churches and ministerial fellowships
1960	Charismatic	Renewal of all restored truth to past movements. *Pastors* were restored as sovereign heads of their local churches.	Charismatic churches and charismatic groups within denominational churches
1970	Faith	Faith confessions, prosperity, victorious attitude and life. *Teacher* reestablished as a fivefold minister.	Faith and Word churches

Approximate Year	Movement	Major Truths Restored	Denominations Founded
1980	Prophetic	Personal prophecy, activation gifts, warfare praise, prophets to nations. *Prophet* ministry was restored and a company of prophets brought forth.	Prophetic churches and networks
1990	Apostolic	Apostolic leadership, release of miracles, networking, great harvest. *Apostle* ministry restored to bring divine order, finalize restoration of fivefold ministers for full equipping of the saints.	Apostolic churches and networks
2007	Saints	Saints demonstrating the Gospel of the Kingdom and reaping the harvest.	Seven-mountain saints and kingdom influencers
2008	Third Reformation	Fulfillment of all things.	Thy Kingdom come
2016	Army of the Lord	God's mighty warriors.	Transformation of nations, sheep and goat nations, God's WWIII

and His Church army have established God's Kingdom over all the earth (see Hebrews 1:13; 10:12–13; Numbers 14:21; Isaiah 11:9; Ephesians 1:12; Revelation 11:15).

We must keep in mind that Jesus promised all of His overcoming sons and daughters that they would become joint heirs of Christ and co-laborers with Him now and in all that He shall ever be and do throughout eternity (see Romans 8:17; 1 Thessalonians 4:16–17). We do not, however, know how much can be accomplished while the Church is still mortal and how much must wait to be accomplished until the Church is immortalized after being resurrected and translated. That is yet to be determined.

The earth is the Lord's and the fullness thereof (Psalm 24:1)—some translations say that the earth and everything in it belongs to the Lord Jesus. And everything the Father gave Jesus, He has given to His Church. "As the Father has sent Me," He said, "I also send you [with the same commission]" (John 20:21). Jesus declared that all power in heaven and earth was given to Him, and He has given all that power and authority to His Church: "Go, therefore, with all that has been given to you," He was saying, "and preach My Gospel and demonstrate My Kingdom" (see Matthew 28:18–20; John 17:18; Luke 10:19; 1 John 3:8).

Jesus' Personal Body and Corporate Body

Acts 3:21 emphatically declares that Jesus cannot return for His second coming to earth until all prophetic Scriptures are fulfilled. It is important to note that Jesus has already fulfilled the Scriptures concerning the coming of the Messiah. When Jesus came from heaven to earth and took upon Himself a human body, He had to fulfill many prophecies in that body before He could return to heaven. This He did through His life, death and resurrection. As He hung on the cross, dying, He cried out, "It is finished," and in His prophetic prayer in John 17:4, He declared that He had finished the work His Father had given Him to do in His mortal body on earth.

Peter confirmed in Acts 3:18 that Jesus was the true Messiah and that He fulfilled all Messianic prophecies. The last major Messianic prophecy Jesus fulfilled was the one David spoke: that God would not allow the body of His Holy One to see corruption (see Psalm 16:10). Jesus fulfilled this Scripture when God raised His body from the dead, transforming it into an incorruptible, immortal human body. When Jesus moved back into His resurrected human body, it made Him a whole man again, with a spirit, soul and body, as all His saints will have throughout eternity. He will always be God's perfect man and man's perfect God.

Father God then said to Jesus, "Sit at my right hand, until I make your enemies a footstool for your feet" (Hebrews 1:13). Jesus "sat down at the right hand of God, from that time waiting till His enemies are made His footstool" (Hebrews 10:12–13). Who is Jesus waiting on to make His enemies His footstool? The one He gave all of His power and authority to, whom He commissioned to fulfill this decree: Jesus' anointed one, His Church. On earth Jesus fulfilled all prophetic Scriptures concerning the Messiah in His personal body; He has now commissioned His corporate Body, still on earth, to fulfill the remaining prophetic Scriptures up to His second coming.* All remaining prophetic Scriptures Jesus will fulfill in and through His corporate Body, His victorious Church.

Jesus has longed to return to resurrect and translate His Church unto Himself ever since He left. He knows, however, that the Church has to grow in number, grow in grace and

* In chapter 16 of my book on the Third Church Reformation, *Prophetic Scriptures Yet to Be Fulfilled*, I reveal sixteen sets of Scripture that must be fulfilled before heaven can release Jesus to come back.

knowledge, demonstrate all truth and fulfill every purpose God has for the Church on earth before that burning desire can be fulfilled. Therefore Jesus patiently waits for the early- and latter-rain outpouring to bring His Church to harvest time.

Scriptures Fulfilled by the Army of the Lord

Before we say any more, let us examine the Scriptures that verify this truth and destiny for the Church. Hear with a believing heart what God has to say to His end time saints who are preparing to be warriors in His army.

> Let the saints be joyful in glory; let them sing aloud on their beds. Let the high praises of God be in their mouth, and a two-edged sword in their hand, to execute vengeance on the nations, and punishments on the peoples; to bind their kings with chains, and their nobles with fetters of iron; *to execute on them the written judgment—this honor have all His saints.* Praise the LORD!
>
> Psalm 149:5–9

Called to Reign

When Daniel saw the vision of future earthly kingdoms that would come into conflict with the Kingdom of God, he was also shown that the saints of God would ultimately prevail and rule:

> *A judgment was made in favor of the saints* of the Most High, and the time came for the saints to possess the kingdom. . . . "Then the kingdom and dominion, and the greatness of the *kingdoms under the whole heaven, shall be given to* the people, *the saints* of the Most High. His kingdom is an everlasting kingdom, and all dominions shall serve and obey Him."
>
> Daniel 7:22, 27

Called to Execute Judgment

Enoch, born in the 622nd year after Adam, walked perfectly with God and ultimately defeated the angel of death for his personal life; this was the original translation, a precursor of what will happen to the saints at Jesus' return. Enoch prophetically saw Jesus' Church judging the nations:*

> Now Enoch, the seventh from Adam, prophesied about these men also, saying, "Behold, the Lord comes with *ten thousands of His saints*, to *execute judgment on all*, to convict all [like judges convicting and sentencing criminals] who are ungodly among them of all their ungodly deeds which they have committed in an ungodly way, and of all the harsh things which ungodly sinners have spoken against Him."
>
> Jude 14–15

In the New Testament, Paul confirms that the Church saints will have the same ministry of judgment: "Do you not know that *the saints will judge the world*? And if the world will be judged by you, are you unworthy to judge the smallest matters? Do you not know that *we shall judge angels*?" (1 Corinthians 6:2–3; Paul is speaking of the angels who fell with Lucifer, who became Satan).

Called to Overcome

Jesus confirms that the right to execute His eternal judgments and rule is given to His overcoming saints:

* Enoch also prophetically saw the judgment of God to be executed through the Flood. He was 65 when his son Methuselah was born. That is probably when Enoch made the prophecy recorded in Jude 14–15, for he named his son, "When he is gone, judgment will come." Enoch was translated to heaven without dying in the 987th year after Adam, which was around 5,000 years ago. Methuselah was born in the 687th year and died at age 969, in the same year the Flood came (1,656 years after Adam). Possibly one of the last official ceremonies Noah performed just before he went into the Ark was the funeral of his grandfather, Methuselah—"For when he is gone, judgment will come."

And he who overcomes, and keeps My works until the end, to him I will give power over the nations—"He [the overcomer] shall rule them with a rod of iron; they shall be dashed to pieces like the potter's vessels"—as I also have received from My Father; and I will give him [the overcomer] the morning star. He who has an ear, let him hear what the Spirit says to the churches.

Revelation 2:26–29

To him who overcomes I will grant to sit with Me on My throne, as I also overcame and sat down with My Father on His throne. He who has an ear, let him hear what the Spirit says to the churches.

Revelation 3:21–22

Called to Conquer

Look with your spiritual eyes and see what John saw in the heavenlies as he wrote his revelation of Jesus Christ:

Behold, a white horse. He who sat on it had a bow; and a crown was given to him, and he went out *conquering and to conquer*.

Revelation 6:2

Behold, a white horse. And He who sat on him was called Faithful and True, and in righteousness *He judges and makes war.* . . . On His head were many crowns. . . . He was clothed with a robe dipped in blood. . . . And the armies in heaven, clothed in fine linen [the righteousness of the saints], white and clean, followed Him on white horses. Now out of His mouth goes a sharp sword, that with it He should strike the nations. And He Himself will rule them with a rod of iron. He Himself treads the winepress of the fierceness and wrath of Almighty God. And He has on His robe and on His thigh a name written: KING OF KINGS AND LORD OF LORDS.

Revelation 19:11–16

Jesus will not return to earth to make peace; He is returning to take over. As His army, we are called to join in His victory as we follow our Commander in Chief, for "we are more than conquerors through Him" (Romans 8:37).

Called to War

The prophet Joel also prophesied about the invincible, unstoppable army of the Lord (see Joel 2:1–13, 28–29). This is a dualistic and progressive prophecy. In Acts 2:16–18, the apostle Peter recognized that what happened on the day of Pentecost was a direct fulfillment of what Joel had prophesied.* It was, however, fulfilled only in part; it will ultimately be fulfilled when God's army is manifested during the army of the Lord movement. It will also be fulfilled by and through natural Israel and at the same time be fulfilled spiritually by and through Christ's Church. Below I explain various facets of the fulfillment of Joel 2:1–11:

> "Blow the trumpet in Zion, and sound an alarm in My holy mountain!" This is God's Church, as described in Isaiah 2:2–3.
>
> "Let all the inhabitants of the land tremble; for the *day of the LORD* is coming, for it is at hand." On this day He comes to be glorified in His saints (see 2 Thessalonians 1:10).
>
> "A day of darkness and gloominess, a day of clouds and thick darkness, like the morning clouds spread over the

---

* Peter brought up Joel's prophecy in response to the crowd's amazement that the disciples were speaking in tongues. Though Joel's prophecy does not say anything about speaking in other tongues, Isaiah prophesied a manifestation of God's Word delivered to unbelieving Israel through a foreign tongue in Isaiah 28:11. Isaiah was prophesying about God bringing forth a nation to bring judgment upon Israel, who would speak in a strange manner, with stuttering lips, when they tried to communicate with Israel. Paul used this Scripture in 1 Corinthians 14:21 to validate the experience of Christian saints speaking with other tongues when they receive the gift of the Holy Spirit.

mountains." This is a day of darkness for the world but the dawning of a new day for the Church.

"A fire devours before them. . . . Surely nothing shall escape them. . . . Like the noise of a flaming fire that devours the stubble, like a strong people set in battle array." God's fiery warriors devour the wicked, like the stubble devoured by the fire (see Malachi 4:1).

"They *run like mighty men*, they climb the wall like *men of war*; every one marches in formation." They will know and be faithful in their membership ministries.

"They do not break ranks." They are submissive and consistent in their calling.

"They do not push one another." They walk in unity and love.

"Every one marches in his own column"—maintaining their positions and performance.

"Though they lunge between the weapons, they are not cut down." This is death to self, fullness of life and one with God's Word. The King James Version words it this way: "When they fall upon the sword [God's Word], they shall not be wounded."

"They run to and fro. . . . The *earth quakes before them*, the heavens tremble. . . . *The* LORD *gives voice before His army*, for His camp is very great; for *strong is the One who executes His word*."

Proclaim this among the nations: "*Prepare for war!* Wake up the mighty men, let all the *men of war* draw near, let them come up. Beat your plowshares into *swords* and your pruning hooks into *spears* [that which was used to plow and bless will now be turned into weapons of war]; let the weak say, 'I am strong.'" Assemble and come, all you nations, and gather together all around. *Cause Your mighty ones to go down there*, O LORD.

147

"Let the nations be wakened, and come up to the Valley of Jehoshaphat; for there I will sit to judge all the surrounding nations. Put in the sickle, for the harvest is ripe. Come, go down; for the winepress is full, the vats overflow—for their wickedness is great." Multitudes, multitudes in the valley of decision! For the day of the LORD is near in the valley of decision [the greatest harvest of souls ever during this time, and also God's greatest destructive judgments upon the wicked]. The sun and moon will grow dark, and the stars will diminish their brightness. *The LORD also will roar from Zion*, and utter His voice from Jerusalem; the heavens and earth will shake; but the LORD will be a shelter for His people, and the strength of the children of Israel.

Joel 3:9–16

Called to Bring About Babylon's Downfall

Isaiah the son of Amoz saw the burden against Babylon. "Lift up a banner on the high mountain [the Church], raise your voice to them; wave your hand, that they may enter the gates of the nobles. *I have commanded My sanctified ones*; I have also called My mighty ones for My anger—those *who rejoice in My exaltation*." The noise of a multitude in the mountains, like that of many people! A tumultuous noise of the kingdoms of nations gathered together! The LORD of hosts musters the *army for battle*. They come from a far country, from the end of heaven—the LORD and His *weapons of indignation*, to destroy the whole land. Wail, for the day of the LORD is at hand! It will come as destruction from the Almighty [to destroy the wicked and the works of the devil]. . . . *Behold, the day of the Lord comes*, cruel, with both wrath and fierce anger, to lay the land desolate; and He will destroy its sinners from it. . . . "I will punish the world for its evil, and the wicked for their iniquity; I will halt the arrogance of the proud, and will lay low the haughtiness of the terrible. I will make a mortal more rare than fine gold, a man more than the golden wedge of Ophir. Therefore I will shake the heavens,

148

and the earth will move out of her place, in the wrath of the LORD of hosts and in the day of His fierce anger."

Isaiah 13:1–6, 9, 11–13

"You are My battle-ax and weapons of war: For with you I will break the nation in pieces; with you I will destroy kingdoms. . . . And I will repay Babylon and all the inhabitants of Chaldea for all the evil they have done in Zion in your sight," says the LORD. . . . And the land will tremble and sorrow; for every purpose of the LORD shall be performed against Babylon.

Jeremiah 51:20, 24, 29

I saw the woman [Babylon, who rules over the kings of the earth], drunk with the blood of the saints and with the blood of the martyrs of Jesus. . . . "[The kings under Babylon] will make war with the Lamb, and the Lamb will overcome them, for He is Lord of lords and King of kings; and those who are with Him are called, chosen, and faithful." . . . "Therefore [Babylon's] plagues will come in one day—death and mourning and famine. And she will be utterly burned with fire, for strong is the Lord God who judges her. . . . Rejoice over her, O heaven, and you holy apostles and prophets, for God has avenged you on her!" . . . After these things I heard a loud voice of a great multitude in heaven, saying, "Alleluia! Salvation and glory and honor and power belong to the Lord our God! For true and righteous are His judgments, because He has judged the great harlot who corrupted the earth with her fornication; and He has avenged on her the blood of His servants shed by her." Again they said, "Alleluia! Her smoke rises up forever and ever!"

Revelation 17:6, 14; 18:8; 19:1–3

Called to Be Untouchable and Unstoppable

Behold in Scripture the tremendous power and protection that God gives His army. We lay hold of these promises

149

somewhat now, but when the army of the Lord is released and the saints come into their ministry of eternal judgment, these Scriptures will be accomplished in their fullness.

"No weapon formed against you shall prosper, and every tongue which rises against you *in judgment you shall condemn.* This is the heritage of the servants of the LORD, and their righteousness is from Me," says the LORD.

Isaiah 54:17

Behold, *I give you the authority* to trample on serpents and scorpions [the devil and his evil angels], and *over all the power of the enemy* [Satan, whether in the spiritual or natural realm], and *nothing shall by any means hurt you.*

Luke 10:19

Surely He shall deliver you from the snare of the fowler [the cunning devices of the devil] and from the perilous pestilence. He shall cover you with His feathers, and under His wings you shall take refuge [shielded by a force field of God's presence]. . . . *You shall not be afraid* of the terror by night [a secret invasion], nor of the arrow that flies by day [rocket, missile], nor of the pestilence that walks in darkness [germ warfare], nor of the destruction that lays waste at noonday [atomic warfare]. A thousand may fall at your side, and ten thousand at your right hand; but *it shall not come near you* [supernatural protection]. Only with your eyes shall you look, and see the reward of the wicked. . . . *No evil shall befall you,* nor shall any plague come near your dwelling; *for He shall give His angels charge over you,* to keep you in all your ways [a canopy of angels around us like a bubble]. In their hands they shall bear you up, lest you dash your foot against a stone. You shall tread upon the lion [the Devil prowling about as a roaring lion, counterfeit to the Lion of Judah] and the cobra, the young lion and the serpent *you shall trample under foot.* . . . "I will be with him in trouble;

I will deliver him and honor him. With long life [resurrection life] *I will satisfy* him, and *show him My salvation* [deliverance and triumphant victory]."

Psalm 91:3–8, 10–13, 15–16

And I will give *power* to my two witnesses, and they shall prophesy. . . . And if anyone wants to harm them, *fire proceeds from their mouth and devours their enemies*. And if anyone wants to harm them, he must be killed in this manner. *These have power to shut heaven*, so that no rain falls in the days of their prophecy; and they have power over waters to turn them to blood, and *to strike the earth with all plagues, as often as they desire*.

Revelation 11:3, 5–6

Now that is unlimited power! Can you imagine how purified, proven, dead to self and full of Christ's life, perfected in Christ's character, wisdom and maturity, we will have to be before God will entrust such power to us?

God not only gives power and authority to His army, He gives them the assurance that they will be protected against all the horrible weapons of the enemy as they engage in this war of wars. It will be a spiritual battle, but it will be executed by mortal saints who are walking in the first phase of Christ's supernatural resurrection life.

Face-to-Face in the Final Battle

In the final battle for earth, the redeemed righteous in battle array will stand face-to-face against the unredeemed wicked. It will be as when David stood face-to-face against the wicked giant, Goliath. Before the day was over, one of them would lay dead upon the battlefield. But the young David prophesied his enemy's downfall and followed through with his own proven weapon, using it to destroy those who wanted to harm him.

151

He prophesied a divine decree of judgment and then executed God's judgment upon the wicked one. Remember that our weapons of warfare are not carnal but spiritual, with power to destroy principalities and powers (see 2 Corinthians 10:4–6). Though they are spiritual, they are nonetheless weapons for the Church army to use against all its enemies, whether they are natural or spiritual. By the time the army of the Lord movement begins to fully manifest God's glory and judgments (at which point the Church will have begun to fulfill the doctrines of resurrection life and eternal judgment—see Hebrews 6:1–2), the human race will be separated into two camps: those who are divinely possessed and those who are demon possessed.

Jesus Christ, the Commander in Chief of His army, will arise within His Church as a mighty man of war. He will be looking through the eyes of His saints at His enemy, the devil. The great war against the portion of the human race who are demonized will be fought on earth by Christ as head and commander of His Church army. It will be Christ fighting not somewhere in the mystical realm but Christ in us, our hope of glory (see Colossians 1:27). Christ's glory will cover the earth as the waters cover the sea. God almighty will fulfill the sworn oath He made to Himself in Numbers 14:21: "Truly, as I live, all the earth shall be filled with the glory of the Lord." That includes everything being put under the feet of Jesus Christ and every knee bowing, every tongue confessing that Jesus is the only true God and Lord over everything (see Ephesians 1:22; Philippians 2:9–11).

A Movement Now Preparing

On April 20, 1996, a quarter of a million Christians gathered in the United States capital for the Washington for Jesus rally, coordinated by John Gimenez. The platform was erected on the front steps of the U.S. Capitol. Though it rained most of the day,

God's purpose was accomplished. At 8:30 a.m., Cindy Jacobs prayed an intercessory prayer for America through gigantic loudspeakers. I gave a prophetic decree to the nation concerning God's purpose and dealings with the United States: God would move in His goodness, in mercy and in spiritual revival to turn this nation back to God and His righteousness. If the Church and America, however, had not turned as God wanted them to by the year 2001, then He was going to remove some of His protective covering from America. This would cause great calamity and judgment upon the nation. If the Church and the nation did not turn around by God's goodness, then it would turn by His severity (see Romans 11:22).

Some of this prophetic word was fulfilled September 11, 2001, when Muslim terrorists flew planes into the Twin Towers in New York and into the Pentagon in Washington, D.C.

Each group that spoke over the loudspeakers spoke a prophetic sentence concerning a particular work of unrighteousness in the land. Those declarations of "guilty," with a prophetic declaration of destruction on each ungodly situation, were established in the heavenlies; they will be executed on all ungodly things when the army of the Lord movement sweeps the earth.

New recruits are being drafted and trained, and older soldiers and generals are receiving God's new revelations of our weapons of warfare and prophetic-apostolic strategies. God's army cannot fight with the same weapons that past movements fought with, any more than America could fight in a third world war in the natural and win with the same weapons they used in World Wars I and II. Many of the old apostolic generals will have to take time off to be taught the strategies and advanced weapons that will be used in the army of the Lord movement. These generals' old "hard drives" are being rewired and updated with the Holy Spirit's latest technology. They are being purified and tested to see if they are ready to walk in this new revelation. Everything that can be shaken is being shaken so that what cannot be shaken may remain.

The soldiers in this movement must function like a well-oiled machine, everything in perfect working order. Intensified test drives are being made to see if we can take the prolonged pressure and strain of God's spiritual Indianapolis 500. God intends for His racers to be winners. The race is not won by the quick starters but by those who can maintain the right speed, avoid wrecking and not fall apart or break down while pressing on to win the race and receive the prize. The baptism of fire is consuming everything in God's saints that is wood, hay and stubble so that only the golden nature of Jesus Christ remains in our character and ministry (see 1 Corinthians 3:12–15). It is good to know that gold cannot be destroyed by fire; fire can only make it purer. The hotter the fire gets, the purer the gold becomes.

That is the reason God declared that He would take His special chosen ones through seven levels of fire until we become like gold in heaven, which is clear as crystal (see Psalm 12:6; Malachi 3:3). All of the old nature and attitude is burned out; only the clear crystal nature of Jesus Christ will remain. He said He would bring one third through the fire, which refers to the third level of overcomers, those who will love not their lives unto death (Zechariah 13:9; Psalm 11:5; Job 23:10; Hebrews 12:1; Revelation 12:11).

The Church is being prepared, not for a skirmish or little war but for the greatest battle against the final enemy. They are now being equipped with the revelation and powerful authority to go against the most formidable walled fortress that Satan has ever built. Jesus paid the price for the redemption of our bodies as well as our spirits and souls, and He took the keys of death from the devil, bringing them to heaven when He arose. Jesus has already provided everything for the full redemption of your spirit, soul and body. Yet there is no account in Church history of even one member of the Body of Christ being able to appropriate

Christ's victory over death. None of God's saints have gotten out of this world alive in their physical bodies. All have been taken out by the agent of death. Satan is determined that none will leave without dying, but Jesus has other plans (see 1 Corinthians 15:51–54; 2 Corinthians 5:4; 1 Thessalonians 4:13–18; 2 Thessalonians 1:5–11; Psalm 102:18–20; Romans 8:23).

At some point, when God's saints are waging their battle as His army and are establishing His Kingdom on earth, Jesus will arise from His seat at the right hand of the Father. He will leap forth with His sword in His hand and give a shout that rings out to the ends of the universe and all over planet earth. He will shout, "Satan, your time is up! Angel of death, your power over My Church is canceled and destroyed." He will have His archangel sound the trumpet of the Lord as He shouts to His Church: "Delay shall not be one minute longer, for it is time for your final redemption and victory over death!" As He is shouting this, He will descend from heaven faster than the speed of light, bringing with Him all the saints who have lost their bodies to death. As He comes into earth's atmosphere, He will shout again, and in a moment, in the twinkling of an eye, all the bodies of those saints will ascend to meet the Lord and be joined with their spirit beings as their bodies become eternally indestructible. Their bodies will never see death again. Then those saints who have been warring against death will finally win when Christ suddenly changes their bodies from mortal to immortal. Every cell in every body will be changed from corruptible to incorruptible. These saints will meet the Lord in the air, join with saints of all the ages and receive their strategies for finalizing God's purpose for the heavens and the earth.

Why Resurrection and Translation?

We must understand what the resurrection and translation of the saints is *not*. It will not be triggered when a threshold of evil on the earth has been reached. Christ will not be descending like a heavenly helicopter to evacuate the saints out of the battle before they are overrun by the enemy, nor will He return as a heavenly fireman to rescue the saints from a burning world. The resurrection is not the saints being ejected out before the plane crashes or escaping out the back door before the devil breaks down the front door. The activities of some evil beast or antichrist spirit activity do not govern how and when it takes place. Nor is Jesus motivated to take action because of anything that the devil or the world system is doing on earth.

When millions of His saints were being martyred during the first three centuries of the Church, Jesus was not motivated to activate the resurrection and translation. He did not come back for His Church when the great falling away took place during the Dark Ages. These were very negative forces arrayed against and within His Church. Instead, He activated the Second Reformation, mobilizing His Church as a militant army to take back all that was lost during the Dark Ages. This army, which marched under the banner of restoration of truth, has been battling for more than five hundred years; it will not only continue until all truth is restored but also will appropriate the last truth that will enable them to overcome the last enemy (1 Corinthians 15:26).

The resurrection and translation is a positive event that takes place to fulfill God's timely purpose. That purpose is to enable the army of the Lord to finalize the war against all evil. The army of the Lord will progress in the war until they have accomplished all they can in their limited mortal bodies. The resurrection and translation then comes for the purpose of immortalizing their bodies. This will remove all earthly limitations, thereby conferring on the saints unlimited abilities. They will be able to travel in all space realms of the heavenlies just as Jesus and the angels do now. They can move in and out of all dimensions in the natural and spiritual realms, as Jesus did in His resurrected and glorified flesh-and-bone body.

A Ministry to Manifest

This battle can only be won by the last generation of the mortal Church. It is appointed to all humankind to die, but the Scriptures declare that a generation of special people will break the appointment with death: "This will be written for the generation to come . . . to release those appointed to death" (Psalm 102:18, 20). Millions of redeemed saints have an end time destiny to overcome death by participating in Christ's translation. It is no fairy tale—it really is going to happen! Although it has been centuries, in the days of the early Church, since Paul recorded the prophetic promise of the resurrection and translation in 1 Thessalonians 4, it is still on God's agenda. Many preachers have mistakenly announced dates for the resurrection and translation just to see nothing happen, but it is still going to happen to a generation of saints. In Hosea 6:2 the prophet Hosea prophesied that after two days (which, according to 2 Peter 3:8, correspond to two thousand years) God will revive us (full restoration), and on the third day He will raise us up (resurrection).

It is not, however, solely a sovereign act of God; it requires divine revelation and appropriation of faith by the saints. There are two biblical members of this end time company who portray this victory over the last enemy: Enoch and Elijah. Elijah had a revelation that he was going to be taken to heaven without going through the door of death. Enoch had a revelation of the end time when the Lord will come with ten thousands of His saints to execute God's wrath and judgment upon the wicked. This revelation probably included the understanding that God's people would be rescued from death. The Bible declares that "by *faith* Enoch was taken away so that he did not see death" (Hebrews 11:5). This was not a faith revelation without living realities. The Word of God gives testimony that Enoch walked with God and pleased Him in all His ways (see Genesis 5:24; Hebrews 11:5). The resurrection and translation is the fifth of the six doctrines of Christ (see Hebrews 6:1–2). The first four doctrines have required faith, obedience and life participation to appropriate; the last two doctrines will require the same.

One Now and Forever

Romans 5:9 declares that God has not appointed us to receive wrath but to co-labor with Him in executing His wrath upon the wicked of this world (see also Psalm 149:6–9). The victorious, overcoming, last-day army of the Lord will fulfill numerous Scriptures declaring the downfall of Satan and all evil—the fall and destruction of Babylon and the subduing of all enemies under Christ's feet.

Jesus and His Church are now joined together in one universal, many-membered Body of Christ. We are joint heirs and sharers in all that Jesus shall ever do, both now and throughout eternity. Jesus was joined with His Church on the Day of Pentecost, and the two became one corporate Body of Christ—Jesus the Head and many millions of saints the Body. Everything that God eternally ordained for Jesus to be, do and fulfill will be done with His Church. Everything you find Christ doing in the New Testament, including in the book of Revelation, He is doing with His Church. Jesus fulfilled His personal mission in His mortal and resurrected body; now it is His purpose, joy and delight to accomplish and fulfill all remaining things in, through, by and with His Church. It takes nothing from Christ's glory for the Church to be one with Him in all things, for Jesus established the Church "to be to the praise of His glory." The

Church is destined to go from glory to glory until it becomes the personification of His glory—a glorious Church. The Church will always be the main manifestation of His glory, for "unto him be glory in the church by Christ Jesus throughout all ages, world without end" (Ephesians 3:21 KJV). His Church is the glory of the knowledge of the Lord that shall fill and cover the earth as the waters cover the sea. We are being changed from glory to glory until we become His glory that fills the earth, demonstrating the glory of God's Kingdom (see Isaiah 11:9–10; Ephesians 1:12; 3:21; 5:27; 2 Corinthians 3:17–18; Numbers 14:21; Psalm 72:19).

The final restoration move of God shall fill the earth with the Church of the living God and cause all the kingdoms of this world to become the kingdoms of our Lord Jesus and His anointed, joint heir, co-laboring Church.

Millions of Spirit-filled Christians believe there is an active army of the Lord in the Church today. They believe this army has a destiny to execute God's purposes and judgments upon the earth. They have various opinions as to when, where and how this will take place. But there is no question that it is in the plans and purposes of God. Whether people have eschatological beliefs that support post-, mid- or pre-tribulation Rapture, they still believe that God's overcoming Church will be God's warriors who will subdue and destroy all evil off His earth, then rule and reign with Christ over the new earth.

After ministering for more than 64 years, I would love to take a seven-year sabbatical before fighting in the final battle. I would take three and a half years, or even five minutes. But if Jesus chooses to give me only the twinkling of an eye, then I will stay one with my Jesus, a warrior with my mighty warrior King, until all enemies are under His feet and made His footstool.

Whether the process takes seven years, three and a half years, five minutes or one second is not relevant. The fact remains that Jesus has declared that He will bring forth a Church army that will be joint heirs and co-laborers with Him in executing His judgments until all enemies are under His feet, where they are supposed to be. Most of these things will be activated during the army of the Lord movement, when the prepared saints enter into their eternal judgment ministry. This will take place before God's great white throne of judgment, the place of eternal sentencing of the unrighteous and of rewarding the righteous overcomers. Let us press toward the mark for the prize that comes with reaching and fulfilling our high calling of God in Christ Jesus. During the last restoration movements of the mortal Church and into eternity, the sufferings and battles of this present life are not worthy to be compared with the glory that shall be revealed in us (see Romans 8:18; Philippians 3:14).

ENLIGHTENMENT, DECLARATION AND PRAYER

Jesus, Your Word is clear: You have predestined in these last days of the mortal Church that it will become a mighty army of conquerors to destroy Your enemies. Jesus, I want to receive Your spiritual military training so that I can co-labor with You as a mighty warrior in Your spiritual World War III, which will prepare the way for Your Kingdom to come and Your will to be done on earth as it is in heaven (Matthew 6:10; Hebrews 10:12–13).

10

The Eternal Judgment Ministry

As we have seen, the Church-army of the Lord will enter into a last-day ministry before its immortalization and into an even greater ministry afterward. God's ultimate goal for this age is a matured Church with the fullness of Christ's life—an equipped army ready to arise with Christ Jesus to fight and win the greatest battle of the ages.

The Church is destined to experientially manifest the sixth doctrine of Christ, eternal judgment. I spoke of this briefly in the last chapter. The doctrine of the eternal judgment is not the same as the judgment seat of Christ or the judgment before the white throne. Rather I am referring to Christ's judgment of the world and the angels through the Church. "Do you not know that the saints will judge the world? . . . Do you not know that we [the Church] are to judge angels?" (1 Corinthians 6:2–3 RSV).

The doctrine of eternal judgment will be fully manifested when Jesus activates His Church into the army of the Lord and fulfills Revelation 11:15: "The kingdoms of this world have become the kingdoms of our Lord and of His Christ, and He shall reign forever and ever!" This Scripture is applicable both to our

Lord Jesus and His Church, for the Church is Jesus' *christos*, "anointed one," just as Jesus is God's *christos*. This is evident in that the Church is called the Body of Christ; it is the same to say, "the Body of the Anointed," or Jesus' anointed corporate Body. Followers of the Anointed One, *christianos* in Scripture, are called after His name. The Church is one body of believers referred to in the singular, not the plural. It is our Lord's anointed one.

Fulfillment of the Six Doctrines of Christ

In my book *The Eternal Church*, I explain the six doctrines of Christ, which are revealed Hebrews 6:1–2:

> Therefore, leaving the discussion of the elementary principles of Christ, let us go on to perfection, not laying again the foundation of repentance from dead works and of faith toward God, of the doctrine of baptisms, of laying on of hands, of resurrection of the dead, and of eternal judgment.

The following is an adaptation of what I wrote in *The Eternal Church* explaining how Christians are to regard this Scripture.[*]

Six doctrines of Christ are given in Hebrews 6:1–2:

>> repentance from dead works
>> faith toward God
>> doctrine of baptisms
>> laying on of hands
>> resurrection of the dead
>> eternal judgment

There are two hermeneutically acceptable interpretations to this Scripture. The first is a foundational personal application. This

---

[*] Hamon, *The Eternal Church*, 151–156.

interpretation regards Hebrews 6:1–2 as containing the general doctrines of Christian faith for the individual. When one has an understanding of these foundational truths, one can progress to more advanced teachings and to maturity. Some theologians look upon these doctrines of Christ as being similar to the Apostles' Creed, which was the initial confession of a person who was baptized into the Christian Church in the fourth century:

"I believe in God, the Father Almighty, Creator of heaven and earth; and in Jesus Christ, His only Son, Our Lord; Who was conceived by the Holy Ghost, was crucified, died, and was buried. He descended into hell; the third day He arose again from the dead; He ascended into heaven and sitteth at the right hand of God, the Father Almighty; from thence He shall come to judge the living and the dead. I believe in the Holy Ghost, the holy catholic [universal] Church; the communion of saints; the forgiveness of sins; the resurrection of the body; and the life everlasting; Amen."

With this understanding of Hebrews 6:1–2, a person simply repents from his dead works, expresses his faith in a living God, acknowledges his faith in Christ Jesus by baptism in water and in the Holy Spirit, receives the laying on of hands, and confesses his belief in the general resurrection of the dead and the eternal judgment of the wicked at the great Day of Judgment. By going through this process of initiation into the doctrines of Christ, one is brought to a place of perfect standing with God.

These six doctrines are looked upon as the foundation stones of the Christian faith that are to be established in our lives. We then are to "go on to perfection," not continually laying again these same foundational truths of the Christian faith. The Christian walk is not a circle but a straight and narrow way, always going onward and upward.

The second acceptable interpretation of this Scripture is a restorational, corporate application. This is the interpretation emphasized in the restoration of the Church. The arrangement of the six doctrines of Christ in this Scripture was not coincidental; it was divinely inspired by the Holy Spirit. The six doctrines were lost during the dark age of the Church, and they have been in

Table 2. Restoration of the Doctrines of Christ*

Approximate Date	Spiritual Experiences		Doctrine of Christ	Baptism/ Witness	Restoration Movements and Denominations
1500	Justification	• Study of the Word • Prayer • Peace	(1) Repentance from Dead Works Grace and Faith (Eph. 2:8–9)	Blood	Protestant • Lutheran • Episcopal • Presbyterian
1700	Sanctification	• Conviction • Faith • Hymns • Joy • Singing	(2) Faith toward God Divine Healing (Jas. 5:14–15).	Water	Holiness • Baptist • Methodist • All Evangelicals • Church of God • Christian and Missionary Alliance
1900	Manifestation	• Unknown Tongues • Hand Clapping, Shouting • Fasting • Dancing in the Spirit • Musical Instruments	(3) Doctrine of Baptisms Spiritual Gifts (1 Cor. 12:7–11): • Messages in Tongues • Interpretation of Tongues	Spirit	Pentecostal • Assemblies of God • Pent. Holiness • Foursquare • Pent. Church of God • Church of God in Christ
1960	Ministration	• Singing/Praises • Spiritual Songs • Worship • Psalms • Ministry to the Body of Christ • Praise in Dance • Acts of Faith, Arts/Drama	(4) Laying on of Hands Spiritual gifts: • Prophecy • Word of Knowledge • Healing • Word of Wisdom • Faith Laying on of Hands for: • Healing • Deliverance • Holy Ghost • Revealing One's Place in Body of Christ Impartation of Gifts by the Holy Spirit.	Body of Christ	Charismatic • Latter Rain • Discipleship • Faith • Kingdom

In 1988, the prophetic movement was birthed to produce a company of prophets and apostles that would make ready a people and prepare the way for Jesus to return by revealing, restoring and fulfilling the remaining prophetic Scriptures and God's total purpose for His church.

Approximate Date†	Spiritual Experiences	Doctrine of Christ	Baptism/Witness	Restoration Movements and Denominations
20??	Glorification • High Praises • Righteousness • *Agape* Love • Divine Unity	(5) Resurrection of the Dead (First Phase) Spiritual Gifts: • Working of Miracles • Discerning of Spirits Church purified and made spotless, reaching full maturity in Christ. End Result: • Redemption of the body • victory over the last enemy • mortality ended in life	Fire	Body of Christ One United and Perfected Church
20??	Adjudication Sevenfold Spirit	(6) Eternal Judgment • All spiritual gifts and fruits released to the Church. • Manifestation of Joel's army of the Lord and of the sons of God. • Saints execute written judgment.	Love	Army of the Lord • Overcomers • Bride of Christ
20??	Administration	(7) Ultimate perfection • God's Seventh Day of Rest • Thousand-Year Reign of Peace on Earth • Overcomers Reign with Christ	Wisdom	Queen Church God's Kingdom on Earth
Endless Age	Continuation	(8) New Earth and New Heavens • Redemption of Creation • Restoration of the Earth • Church Begins Eternal Ministry	Fullness	Eternal Church Universal Reign

* Based on Hebrews 6:1–2 and Acts 3:21.

† Though we do not know the exact date or time, from my study of Church history and the Lord's revelation through Scripture, I believe the glorification, adjudication, administration and continuation phases of the Church will occur in this century.

the process of being restored to the Church in the same order in which they are listed in Hebrews 6:1–2, as can be seen in Table 2.

The first four doctrines have already been restored, as we see from the history of Christianity during the last five hundred years. They have already brought about major restorational movements and the establishment of new experiential truth to the eternal Church. The context of Hebrews 6:1–2 indicates that when all six doctrines are fully operating in the Church again, a seventh doctrine of Christ—seen in the biblical teaching on perfection—will be made manifest. This seventh doctrine will be ultimate perfection. This will be followed by the creation of "new heavens and a new earth" (Isaiah 65:17, Isaiah 66:22 and 2 Peter 3:13), the beginning of an eternal age that sees the marriage of the Lamb with His pure, spotless Bride.

Lost Doctrines Reestablished. When the writer of Hebrews spoke of "leaving" the discussion of the doctrines of Christ, it is important to understand that from a restorational aspect, one cannot leave something until it has been established—or, in this case, reestablished. The Church of the Dark Ages lost these truths one at a time until the experiential realities of the six doctrines of Christ no longer existed. The Church cannot go on to full maturity until the Holy Spirit reestablishes the foundation upon which the early Church was built.

As an example of this, Solomon built a beautiful Temple for the habitation of God. For years it was a praise to the glory of God. But Israel began to fall away from the faith and finally became an apostate nation, leading to the complete destruction of the Temple by the Babylonians. When the Jews, led by Zerubbabel, returned from their Babylonian captivity, they had to start again with the basics. They had to re-lay the foundation before the Temple could be built.

Consider also the analogy of a person traveling across the United States. If a family wished to travel by automobile in a staight line from California to Florida, they must journey through six states before arriving at the Florida state line. Florida would be the ultimate objective, but there is no way to arrive in Florida until they pass first through Arizona, New Mexico, Texas, Louisiana, Mississippi and Alabama. The pattern of leaving one state to enter the next would have to be followed state by state in a continuous journey from California to Florida.

Similarly, there is no way for a person to travel from an unregenerate state to maturity without incorporating each of the six doctrines of Christ into his life. One must first repent of dead works, leaving behind these dead works when entering into the state of faith toward God, and then going through all the other Christian truths until the state of ultimate perfection is reached. The same holds for the Church. The six doctrines of Christ laid down in Hebrews 6:1–2 reveal the chronological order in which God has restored and is restoring the Church back to divine order and fullness. As can be seen in the Table 3, these same stages were prophesied many times in the history of God's people Israel; this was "written for our admonition, upon whom the ends of the ages have come" (1 Corinthians 10:11).

Waiting on the Church

In chapter 3 we found that, according to Acts 3:21 (TLB), "[Jesus] must remain in heaven until the final recovery of all things from sin, as prophesied from ancient times." All that the fall of man and sin took away from humanity, Jesus, through His Church, shall restore. Jesus Christ, through His death, burial and resurrection, provided all things necessary for His Church to bring about the "recovery of all things." King David provided all things necessary for the building of the Temple, but the actual task of building was turned over to his son, Solomon. Jesus provided the plan and provision for the recovery (restoration) of all things and the building of His Kingdom, but it was turned over to His many-membered corporate Body, the Church, for its fulfillment. David, through death, had to leave his son to work alone, but Jesus, through His death and resurrection came back

Table 3. Church Restoration Movements and the New Testament Restorational Truths They Fulfilled Correlated with Old Testament Historical Events and Types

Church Restoration Movements	Biblical Spiritual Experiences	Doctrines of Christ (Hebrews 6:1–2)	Journeys of the Children of Israel	Ezekiel's Yard of Dry Bones (Ezekiel 37)	Water from the Temple (Ezekiel 47)	Tabernacle of Moses (Exodus 25–40)
Protestant	Justification	(1) Repentance from dead works	Passover	Breath enters the bones	Water depth to ankles	Brazen alter
Holiness	Sanctification	(2) Faith toward God	Banks of Red Sea, waters of Marah	Sinews laid	Water depth to knees	Laver, table of shewbread
Pentecostal	Manifestation	(3) Doctrine of baptisms	Water from the rock	Flesh is formed	Water depth to loins	Candlestick
Charismatic	Ministration	(4) Laying on of hands	Mt. Sinai	Skin covers the bones	Water deep enough to swim in	Five bars, altar of incense
Body of Christ	Glorification	(5) Resurrection of the dead	Crossing the Jordan	The bones live	Life	Veil and coverings
Army of the Lord	Adjudication	(6) Eternal judgment	Conquering Canaan	Exceedingly great army	Miry place judged	Ark and contents
Queen Church	Administration	(7) Ultimate perfection	Canaan conquered	Davidic king and shepherd	Rest and life	Mercy seat
Eternal Church	Continuation	(8) New earth and new heavens	Ruling and occupying Canaan	Tabernacle of God with man	Temple of God with man	New Temple

in the power of His Holy Spirit and is now living and working within His corporate Body.

Because this work of building the Kingdom of God is not yet complete, Jesus—indeed, all of creation—is in a period of waiting. "But this Man [Jesus], after He had offered one sacrifice for sins forever, sat down at the right hand of God, from that time *waiting* till His enemies are made His footstool" (Hebrews 10:12–13). "For the earnest expectation of the creation *eagerly waits* for the revealing of the sons of God" (Romans 8:19). By "sons of God," Paul is speaking here of the mature, fully restored Church, on which all creation is waiting so that the "creation itself [can be] delivered from the bondage of corruption into the glorious liberty of the children of God" (Romans 8:21).

In the Kingdom of God, it takes two to make one. Jesus has fully identified Himself with the Church. He and His Church are one: He is the head and the Church members are the body, bone of His bone and flesh of His flesh. It takes both a head and a body to make a functioning being, and it takes Jesus and His Church to make one functioning ministry. As husband and wife are one flesh in God's sight (see Ephesians 5:30–31), so Jesus and His Church are one in spirit and ministry (see 1 Corinthians 6:17). The Eternal designed it that way, and it is the greatest delight of Jesus for it to be so.

Jesus has already completed His personal part. When Jesus declared, "It is finished," and prayed, "Father, I have finished the work which You gave Me to do," it revealed that Jesus had finished the work that had to be done by Himself alone. Jesus is thrilled that His independent, individual ministry is over forever. Never again will He have to do anything alone. Whatever else is to be done will be done *with* the Church. In his book *Destined for the Throne*, Paul Billheimer emphasizes this point:

> That this is God's glorious purpose for the Church is authenticated and confirmed by the apostle Paul in 1 Corinthians 6:2–3.

"Do ye not know that the saints shall judge the world? . . . Know ye not that we shall judge angels?" This is an earnest of what Jesus meant when He said to His Father, "The glory that You gave Me I have given them" (John 17:22).*

This royalty and rulership is no hollow, figurative or symbolic thing. It is not a figment of the imagination. The Church, the Bride, Jesus' eternal companion, is to sit *with Him* on His throne. If His throne represents reality, then hers is no fantasy. We are joint heirs (see Romans 8:17), and in law a joint heir can do nothing without the other. Neither heir can do anything alone.

Co-Laborers, Together Forever

Jesus Christ purchased His Church to be His co-laborer and His Bride with whom He could be united—one with Him in all that He was, shall ever be or shall ever do. Everything that Jesus will do, from now to eternity, will be done in, through and with His Church. He will never do anything again without His Bride taking part with Him in its fulfillment.

Jesus has eternally joined Himself to His Church. He united Himself with His Church in its origination, and He did not forsake His Bride during her deterioration. He has continued to give Himself to His Church time after time in restoration, and He will continue until she reaches her ultimate destination. Jesus has delegated His power of attorney to His Church for the performance of His eternal purpose. All things yet to be revealed, restored or fulfilled will be accomplished in, by and through His Church. The Church is now functioning as co-executor of His Word and will continue this ministry after the resurrection and translation.

* Paul E. Billheimer, *Destined for the Throne* (Minneapolis: Bethany House, 1996), 26.

Members of Christ's Body, let your heart rejoice and be glad, for the ministry of the Church is destined never to deactivate or end but rather to escalate and begin on a higher realm. The Church is eternal. It will never be dismembered or disbanded but will become more fully united and eternally magnified in its ministry with Christ Jesus. Hallelujah, Amen!

Be convinced, along with the apostle Paul, that the Church can never be separated from its love, life, reality and ministry with Christ Jesus. Paul had the clearest and most complete revelation of the Church of any of the biblical writers. As a member of Christ's great corporate Body, he spoke with great conviction to the Church at Rome concerning the Church's united ministry and relationship with Jesus. "For I am persuaded that neither death nor life, nor angels nor principalities nor powers, nor things present nor things to come, nor height nor depth, nor any other created thing, shall be able to separate us" (Romans 8:38–39).

Absolutely nothing can stop Jesus from ultimately fulfilling His purpose in and through His Church. Death cannot, nothing in life can, demons in hell or the devil himself cannot, not even angels in the heavens can. The Church is so interwoven into every fiber and purpose of Christ's being that all of heaven would have to be ripped apart and the eternal Godhead destroyed in order to separate the Church from Christ. The Church is in the Father's hand, and no man can pluck it out (see John 10:28–29).

Three Doctrines to Be Fulfilled

Since nothing can stop Jesus Christ from fulfilling His purpose in His Church, the last three doctrines of Christ will be fulfilled as surely as the first four have been. Just as the Church has experientially entered into justification, sanctification, manifestation and ministration, it will now begin to enter into its time of glorification, adjudication and administration, followed by continuation into the endless ages to come.

Saints are Christ's living letters (see 2 Corinthians 3:2–3). Since the mortal Church must fulfill all Scriptures pertaining to it before Jesus can return, it is beneficial to look at some Scriptures that should be fulfilled in and through the Church before its translation. The following Scriptures are by no means exhaustive, but hopefully they will motivate Christians to read the Bible with this thought in mind: Is this Scripture an experiential reality within the Church, and if so, is it a living experience in my life? If it is not active in the Church, then begin to pray and believe for it to be activated and fulfilled.

> Behold, I give you the authority . . . over all the power of the enemy, and *nothing shall by any means* hurt you [this is to be fulfilled physically as well as spiritually].
>
> Luke 10:19

> And as you go, preach, saying, "The kingdom of heaven is at hand." Heal the sick, cleanse the lepers, *raise the dead*, cast out demons. Freely you have received, freely give.
>
> Matthew 10:7–8

> As You [Father] sent Me [Jesus] into the world, I also have sent them [the Church] into the world [with the same commission, power and authority].
>
> John 17:18

> Truly, truly, I say to you, He who *believes* in Me, the works that I do, he will do also; and *greater works* than these he will do; because I go to the Father [to send back the Holy Spirit, who will give the saints the power to do these works].
>
> John 14:12

In that day the LORD will defend the inhabitants of Jerusalem [the Church]; the one who is feeble among them in that day shall be like David, and the house of David shall be like God [Jesus].

Zechariah 12:8

Search for more—there are scores of other Scriptures that reveal the power within the Church. A few individuals have learned how to release this power, but the Body of Christ as a whole has not. The Church is operating on candlelight power, not using the Holy Spirit dynamo capable of generating millions of volts of divine power. All of the fruit and gifts of the Holy Spirit and the sevenfold Spirit of God will be activated in the Church during the last days of its mortal ministry in the world.

ENLIGHTENMENT, DECLARATION AND PRAYER

These Scriptures and tables have given me insight into Your overall purpose for the Holy Spirit's work in and through Christ's Church. Lord Jesus, I want to be a participant of Your present purpose for Your Church. I want to be a Third-Reformation reformer and a warrior in God's World War III. I want to be alive and active at the beginning of the fulfillment of the sixth doctrine of Christ, the saints executing the judgment written in Your Word (Psalm 149:6–9).

11

Divine Decrees as Weapons of War

Divine decrees are those spoken with prophetic revelation and apostolic authority. Decrees that produce that which was decreed are spoken by mature Christians who are biblically knowledgeable and know the voice and timing of the Lord. They have the mind of Christ and the *rhema* word of the Lord in their mouths. They have a relationship with God that gives them confidence to speak with full faith, without doubting.

Decrees do not work for Christians who are immature, self-assuming or unenlightened and who speak their decrees presumptuously. The exception would be a person who has these failings of character but also has a gift of faith that enables him or her to speak with authority and confidence. Jesus declared to His followers,

> Have faith in God. For assuredly, I say to you, whoever says [decrees] to this mountain, "Be removed and be cast into the sea," and does not doubt in his heart, but believes that those

things he says [decrees] will be done, he will have whatever he says [decrees].

Mark 11:22–23

Decrees in the Bible

God decreed that He was going to make a new creation called Man. He decreed He was going to make man in His own image and likeness. He then began the process of fulfilling that decree. He had to first take six days to prepare earth to be man's home. God also planned to make man's body from the substance of the earth—dust, soil and dirt from the ground. He breathed into man a portion of His breath, which created an eternal spirit within the body of man. God then made Adam a comparable and compatible helpmate from a substance from Adam's body. He planted the couple in a beautiful park that would be their home and named it the Garden of Eden. From the first decree in all of time, we can learn how the process works: A divine decree is made, and then God begins the process of making it possible for it to become reality.

Job 22:28 says this about decrees: "You will also declare a thing, and it will be established for you; so light will shine on your ways." The King James Version has, "Thou shalt also *decree* a thing . . ." To decree a thing, you should verbally declare it. In the Old Testament the word *decree* is used numerous times. But only people in high positions with delegated authority, such as kings and governors, made decrees. King Cyrus made a decree for the rebuilding of Jerusalem. Esther received favor from the king to write a decree that saved her people from being slaughtered. The dictionary defines *decree* as "an ordinance or edict promulgated by civil or other authority" and "an authoritative decision." In a law context, it can refer to a judicial decision; it can also refer to a foreordained, eternal purpose of God. Job 22:28 says that when you decree a thing, light will shine on your ways; that means the light of understanding and wisdom will be given for you to understand the process and strategy for bringing it into literal fulfillment.

The biblical use of the word *declare* means to make known, to speak forth, to reveal or to declare something. Like decrees, declarations can be made verbally or through writing. For our study on decrees as weapons of warfare, we will emphasize the emphatic and authoritative speaking forth of decrees.

"I Will Build My Church"

Jesus made a decree in Matthew 16:18 that He would build His Church. This is a good example of the process by which decrees are fulfilled. Before that decree could begin to be fulfilled, Jesus had to first purchase His Church with His own life's blood (see Acts 20:28). Then Jesus had to birth His Church on the Day of Pentecost by His Holy Spirit. The Holy Spirit then gifted each believer with his or her own spirit language, which fulfilled the command of Jesus that they receive the promise of the Father (see Acts 1:4–5; 2:4, 17). In my book *Seventy Reasons for Speaking in Tongues*, I give many reasons why the Holy Spirit chose this gift of speaking in other tongues or a spirit language to be the greatest and most profitable gift He could possibly give to the members of Christ's Church. Father God's greatest gift was His only begotten Son, whom He gave for mankind to be redeemed. Jesus gave His greatest gift to His Church, which was the Holy Spirit. The Holy Spirit's greatest gift was for the individual believer to supernaturally receive his or her own spirit language. *Seventy Reasons for Speaking in Tongues* gives fifteen biblical proofs that this gift was intended for every believer throughout the age of the mortal Church. It also gives thirty personal benefits and twenty-five powerful ministry reasons. If a person has received Father God's gift of His Son for eternal life and has received Jesus' gift of the Holy Spirit, then that person should also receive the Holy Spirit's gift of a personal, supernatural spirit language. This is a vital tool Jesus had the Holy Spirit give to His Church members for fulfilling His decree that He would build His Church—for 1 Corinthians 14:4 and Jude 20 declare that those who pray in their other tongues build themselves up in the most holy faith and keep themselves in the love of God.

After Jesus purchased and birthed the Church, He ascended to heaven and sat down at the right hand of His Father. Jesus then took all of His anointing, attributes and grace for building His Church and divided them into five different ministry gifts (Ephesians 4:11). He gave each of these five Church-building gifts a name:

Apostle

Prophet

Evangelist

Pastor

Teacher

Those who were appointed to these roles were to equip the members of the Church in their membership ministries (verse 12). Their ministries to the saints were to continue until every member of the Body of Christ was built into his or her membership ministry, placed, activated and functioning. This process was to continue until the Body of Christ became "a perfect man, to the measure of the stature of the fullness of Christ" (verse 13). It has continued for nigh unto two thousand years. A certain number and quality of members is needed to make the Body of Christ God's perfect man (see Revelation 6:11). Nothing can stop Christ's decree from being fulfilled in its fullness; Jesus will build His Church to the pattern and finished design He had in mind when He purchased and birthed it (see Matthew 16:18). It would be more glorious and beneficial to Jesus than Solomon's Temple. "Christ also loved the church and gave Himself for her, that He might . . . present her to Himself a glorious church" (Ephesians 5:25–27).

Now is the time to train the warriors who will fight in God's World War III. It is now God's timely purpose for the Church to be trained and equipped to be God's end time army to fulfill God's final purpose for His mortal Church. The saints are to be fully clothed with the whole armor of God and then be educated, trained and activated in their weapons of war. Those called to be warriors on the front line of battle are to be trained like U.S. Marines, Navy SEALs and David's thirty mighty warriors.

We are now living in the time of fulfillment of all the prophetic Scriptures concerning God's end time army of the Lord. Jesus is activating and empowering His army to go on the offensive to fulfill God's purpose for His World War III, just as Jesus and His special force of saints fulfilled God's purposes for His World Wars I and II.

Weapons of War

In Matthew 16:18–19 Jesus decreed that after He built His Church to the degree that He ordained, the gates of hell would no longer be able to prevail against His mature, victorious warrior Church. Jesus would give special keys of the Kingdom of heaven to His generals and commanders directing the war. Whatever these apostolic-prophetic generals and warriors decreed should be bound on earth would be bound in heaven, and whatever they decreed should be loosed on earth would be loosed in heaven. Their power and authority in that day is typified by the ministry of the two witnesses in Revelation 11:

I will give power to my two witnesses, and they will prophesy
. . . if anyone wants to harm them, fire proceeds from their
mouth and devours their enemies . . . these have power to shut
heaven, so that no rain falls in the days of their prophecy; and
they have power over waters to turn them to blood, and to strike
the earth with all plagues, as often as they desire.

Revelation 11:3, 5–6

Jesus demonstrated to His disciples the power of speaking
a decree and then explained how it works:

Now in the morning, as He returned to the city, He was hun-
gry. And seeing a fig tree by the road, He came to it and found
nothing on it but leaves, and said [decreed] to it, "Let no fruit
grow on you ever again." Immediately the fig tree withered away.

And when the disciples saw it, they marveled, saying, "How
did the fig tree wither away so soon?"

So Jesus answered and said to them, "Assuredly, I say to you,
if you have faith and do not doubt, you will not only do what
was done to the fig tree, but also if you say to this mountain, 'Be
removed and be cast into the sea,' it will be done. And whatever
things you ask in prayer, believing, you will receive."

Matthew 21:18–22

Jesus decreed that the tree would never again bear fruit, and
immediately it withered and died. Jesus revealed the working
principle that you must speak in full faith without having the
slightest doubt. How does a Christian develop that kind of
faith? Jesus conveyed to the disciples that if they had a relationship with Him as He has with His Father, they would have
the full assurance and confidence that whatever they decreed,
He would make it happen for them. For whatever you decree
in prayer, believing, you will receive it. I use the word *decree*
for the word *asking* because biblical asking is more than just

requesting the Lord to give you something or do something for you. To *ask* includes *a*sking, *s*eeking and *k*nocking (see Matthew 7:7–8).

Speaking decrees *in* Jesus' name works. Jesus stated that whatever we ask the Father *in* Jesus' name, He would do it. Asking or decreeing something in the name of Jesus, however, is more than just saying the name Jesus. In John 15:7 Jesus declared, "If you abide in Me, and My words abide in you, you will ask what you desire, and it shall be done for you." It is not just saying the name Jesus but abiding *in* Jesus. There is no magic power in just saying the name. Even though the name of Jesus has been exalted above every other name and all hell fears the One that name represents, the secret to the power is being *in* Christ when we use the name of Jesus. When the apostle Paul was ministering in Ephesus, seven sons of a chief priest thought there was magic power in the name of Jesus. They sought to cast demons out of a man by saying, "By the name of Jesus that Paul preaches: Demons, come out" (see Acts 19:13). The demons did not come out; instead they arose within the demoniac, who beat the men up and ran them off. Jesus said that if we abide *in* Him and He *in* us, we could ask whatever we desired and it would be done. It is like saying you can do this or that while you are *in* a jet warplane or a big war tank. You must be *in* Christ and Christ must be abiding *in* you for decrees to really work. When we are really *in* His name and character, and when we have a close relationship with Jesus as He had with His Father, then we can ask and receive or decree and it will be established.

What Power Is in Spoken Decrees?

When we speak words that are in alignment with the mind of Christ and the will of God, we are speaking the words of Christ

Jesus, who was the living Word of God walking planet earth. The body of Jesus was the Word made flesh:

> In the beginning was the Word, and the Word was with God, and the Word was God. . . . And the *Word became flesh* and dwelt among us, and we beheld His glory, the glory as of the only begotten of the Father, full of grace and truth. . . . All things were made through Him [the Word], and without Him [the Word] nothing was made that was made. In Him [the Word] was life.
>
> John 1:1, 14, 3–4 KJV

"For the word of God is *living and powerful*" (Hebrews 4:12). Jesus was the Word of God revealed through His human body. Today we have the Word of God revealed to us through a book, the Bible. God honors and backs up the written Word just as He did Jesus the living Word. The Word of God is still alive and powerful for those who believe and obey it. In fact, Jesus said His Words are *spirit and life* (see John 6:63).

In the beginning God decreed to the heavens and the earth, and they formed into the natural universe and planet earth. The Word spoke again, causing all living things on earth to come into natural existence. God decreed, "Let Us make man in Our own image and likeness." God fulfilled His own decree by forming man's body from the dust of the earth and then breathing an eternal spirit into the body, causing him to come alive in a natural body. A decree is declared and the process begins, causing it to be established and fulfilled as spoken.

The Secret

The secret to getting a spoken decree to work is making sure it is a living *rhema* word of the Lord. Remember that a *rhema* word is a Scripture that is quickened to us, a thought from the mind of Christ or a divine unction from the Holy Spirit. It is not what we feel when we make a decree that is important but what we know and believe.

Man was made different from the animals in several ways, but there are two major ways we want to emphasize in our discussion of words. Man was made with an eternal spirit life within his natural body by God breathing a part of His eternal breath/Spirit into man. Animals were created with the ability to breathe in the air and function as living creatures, but God did not personally breathe His life into them. Therefore, the animals do not have an eternal spirit life within their natural bodies. When they die, they are no more, for they only have natural life. But man himself is a spirit being living in a natural body. When man's natural body dies, his spirit being continues to live on throughout eternity in heaven or hell.

The other major difference is that man can talk. Man was made with the godlike ability to talk and have a creative mind, which God told Adam to use to name all of God's created beings on earth. Adam was created as a grown man, not a baby. He did not have to learn to walk and talk. He immediately could walk with his Creator in the Garden and carry on an intelligent conversation with Him. The natural creation—animals, birds and fish—has ways of communicating through certain sounds and movements, but these creatures do not have the power of speech. Speech makes man special in all creation. Animals do not advance in knowledge like man. Man has advanced from the Stone Age to flying through the air in planes, traveling a mile per minute in cars and trains and traveling underwater like fish, in man-made submarines. Man has increased his ability to communicate in myriad ways, from telegraph to telephone to radio to television to cell phones to the internet. We have used our power of words to record history in volumes that fill libraries; we have written our thoughts and creative ideas in millions of books, made all the easier with electronic publishing. Mankind did not evolve from animals, plants and lower life-forms. He was created an intelligent, walking and talking grown man at the beginning of days.

When we talk about a person using words for speech, communication and creating things, we are talking about a creative, godlike ability that God conferred on man when He made him in His own likeness and image. When we talk about the Word of God, we are referring to the Word that created all things, including heaven, the universe and planet earth. The Word is life giving, self-germinating, creative, all-powerful—the most powerful force in the whole of God's creation. Everything that now exists throughout the universe and eternity came into being because of the Word. That Word of the Gospel is the power of God unto salvation (see Romans 1:16). The Word created all things by His spoken words (see John 1:1–3). So when we speak of the power of words, we are speaking of the potential power of unlimited possibilities. Jesus declared that if we can believe His words, then all things are possible to those who believe and decree His words of promise (see Mark 9:23).

David's Prophetic Decrees in Warfare

The young man David, a shepherd boy at the time, was sent by his father to take food to his three older brothers fighting for Saul in his army. When he arrived, he discovered that Saul and his army of three thousand men had been challenged for forty days by a lone giant of the Philistines. The giant had presented a proposition to Saul: He would fight one of Saul's warriors in the valley between the two armies. If Saul or his champion warrior won, the Philistines would become subject to Israel, but if the giant won, then Israel would become subject to the Philistines.

Just as David was delivering the food, Goliath came forward, roaring his challenge: *"Send me a man!"* The Bible says Saul and his army shivered in fear and drew back from the roar of the giant. David inquired what would be done for the man who went out against the giant and destroyed him. The answer: the king would shower him with great riches, he could marry the king's daughter and his whole family would be exempt from paying taxes.

When David's brothers heard David asking questions, they rebuked him and accused him of being proud and insolent. David replied, "Is there not a cause?" (1 Samuel 17:29). What he was saying was this: Goliath is not defying just any army; he is defying the army of the living God! I will go and kill him! When David was brought before Saul, Saul warned him, "You are but a youth! But this Goliath has been a trained warrior since his youth." But Saul finally commissioned him to go, after David made his prophetic declaration of faith:

> "Your servant has killed both lion and bear; and this uncircumcised Philistine will be like one of them, seeing he has defied the armies of the living God." Moreover David said, "The LORD, who delivered me from the paw of the lion and from the paw of the bear, He will deliver me from the hand of this Philistine."
> . . . Then he took his staff in his hand; and he chose for himself five smooth stones from the brook, and put them in a shepherd's bag, in a pouch which he had, and his sling was in his hand. And he drew near to the Philistine.
>
> 1 Samuel 17:36–37, 40

What a contrast! The giant Goliath was ten feet tall, with a bronze helmet and bronze coat of mail that weighed more than David. His twelve-foot-long spear had an iron head that weighed fifteen pounds, and his shield was broader and taller than David, who was not even six feet tall. David was dressed in casual work clothes—no sword, just his shepherd's staff and slingshot in his hands. Goliath saw him coming and was insulted and infuriated that Saul was sending a youth out to fight him with just a staff. The gigantic, monstrous warrior cursed David and declared he would feed David to the birds, but David countered with his own prophetic warfare decree:

> You come to me with a sword, with a spear, and with a javelin. But I come to you in the name of the LORD of hosts, the God of the armies of Israel, whom you have defied. This day the LORD will deliver you into my hand, and I will strike you and take your head from you. And this day I will give the carcasses of the camp of the Philistines to the birds of the air and the wild beasts of the earth, that all the earth may know that there is a God in Israel. Then all this assembly shall know that the LORD does not save with sword and spear; for the battle is the LORD's, and He will give you into our hands.
>
> 1 Samuel 17:45–47

David moved toward the giant to fulfill his prophetic decree. He put a stone into his slingshot and hurled it straight toward the forehead of Goliath. The stone sank into his forehead and penetrated his brain. That giant collapsed face forward to the ground. I think David shouted, "Thank you, Lord, for the bigger they are, the harder they fall!" The man who had been carrying Goliath's shield dropped it and ran. David ran to the fallen body, pulled the giant's sword out of its sheath and sliced off the head. David no doubt grabbed the ugly head of the giant, blood pouring out, and lifted it up, shouting to Saul and his army, "God has given us the victory! Now let us pursue, kill them and drive them from our land!" God fulfilled David's decree and gave all Israel a victory.

It became a day of rejoicing and victory for God's people. After the battle was over, David took the armor and sword of Goliath and put it in his tent, probably along with the mounted lion and bear that he had killed before, which had prepared him for this victory.

God is bringing forth an army of David-like warriors who are fearless and bold and who know their God and trust Him completely. They will passionately declare, "Is there not a cause?" They will have had experiences of killing their lions and bears and are confident that God will fight for and with them when they go against God's enemies who are defying His army of saints.

Others Who Made Decrees

We find many others in Scripture who made decrees or received them from God. Some of them never saw the results of these decrees; others saw them begun or even fulfilled in their lifetimes. Some have yet to be fulfilled even now.

> **Enoch.** The prophet Enoch made a decree that God was going to come from heaven with ten thousands of His saints to execute judgment upon all the ungodly on the earth (see Jude 14–15). Though his prophecy was decreed more than five thousand years ago, it is yet to be fulfilled. It will be fulfilled during the climax of God's World War III at the end of the Third Reformation.

> **Noah.** When God spoke to Noah, Noah decreed God's word that the end of the world was coming soon to all people (see Genesis 6:13). God was going to send a flood to destroy all living things on the earth. God decreed to Noah to build an Ark to preserve just a few humans to continue the human race on earth. This decree was fulfilled a hundred years later when Noah finished the Ark and brought his family on board, along with a sampling of all land and air creatures on the earth.

> **Abraham.** God decreed for Abraham to start a special race of mankind for God's divine purpose (see Genesis 12:1–4).

187

It was decreed that he would be a father of nations. His descendants would possess a certain land, Canaan, that would become their national heritage. Finally, his seed would bless the world. After the decree was made, it took 25 years for Abraham to become father of a promised son, more than 500 years for his descendants to possess Canaan and make it the nation of Israel and 2,000 years before Jesus Christ the promised seed blessed the world.

Samuel. God spoke to the prophet Samuel to decree to David that he was destined to be king over all Israel, to be a man and king after God's own heart and to fulfill God's prophetic purpose (see 1 Samuel 16:1–13). This process took roughly 24 years: He was around 13 when Samuel anointed him, 30 when he became king over Judah, and 37 when he became king over the united kingdom of Israel (see 2 Samuel 5:4–5). It was another 20 to 30 years before David extended the borders of Israel to their prophesied locations (see Genesis 15:18).

Jeremiah, Isaiah and many Old Testament prophets. Jeremiah prophetically decreed that Israel would be taken to Babylon for 70 years of captivity (Jeremiah 25:11; 29:10). Isaiah prophesied a decree that a king of Persia named Cyrus would be the one who would allow them to return (Isaiah 45:1, 13). The prophet Daniel discovered 68 years later, while studying the book of Jeremiah, that it was about time for the 70 years to be fulfilled (Daniel 9:2). When Cyrus became king of Persia, he decreed Israel's return to rebuild the city of Jerusalem and the Temple. "The elders of the Jews built, and they prospered through the prophesying of Haggai the prophet and Zechariah the son of Iddo" (Ezra 6:13; see also Haggai 1:12).

Archangel Gabriel. Gabriel prophetically decreed that Mary would be made pregnant by almighty God and birth a son who was to be called the Son of God (Luke 1:31–35). The fullness of time had come, and Gabriel spoke with the voice of heaven to decree that it was time for the Messiah to be manifest on the earth. Thirty years later Jesus fulfilled the decree and was manifest on earth as the Messiah (Galatians 4:4).

Jesus Christ. Jesus made a number of prophetic declarations. He decreed, "The time is fulfilled, and the kingdom of God is at hand. Repent, and believe in the gospel" (Mark 1:15). He prophetically decreed that Jerusalem would be destroyed and the Temple torn down, leaving not one stone upon another (Luke 19:44). This was fulfilled 40 years later in AD 70. He also decreed in Matthew 16:18, "I will build My church"—not just birth it and bless it, but *build* the Church to the place it could fulfill its purpose for being built, especially during the Third Church Reformation and God's World War III.

The practice of making prophetic decrees has been continued by the saints since the beginning of the Church. God gave a very important decree through Martin Luther, who had received a major revelation from God. Luther received this revelation from his study and through preaching of the Scriptures: that many of the practices and teachings of the Catholic Church, of which he was a pastor and university professor, were contrary to the Word of God. He wrote 95 arguments against these false teachings and practices and spread them publicly. He declared that a person is righteous before God by faith in Jesus and the blood He shed on the cross, without any of the dead works of praying to Mary, doing penance, etc. Hundreds of books have been written covering all that transpired at that time, and I dedicate numerous pages in my book on Church restoration, *The Eternal Church*, to this very important time in Church history, which was the beginning of the Second Reformation.

The main thing that caused the Pope to have Martin Luther excommunicated from the Church and declared a heretic was his teaching on justification by faith and priesthood of the believer. Years later, Church historians set the date of October 31, 1517, when Martin Luther nailed his 95 Theses to the door of his church in Wittenberg, Germany, as the official beginning of the Protestant movement and the beginning of the biblically prophesied period of restoration, which Peter declared would have to be fulfilled before Jesus could return. God the Father will send Jesus Christ back to earth again, "whom heaven must receive [retain, keep, hold] until the times of *restoration* of all things, which God has spoken by the mouth of all His holy prophets since the world began" (Acts 3:21).

God has certain times to reveal and make known certain mysteries that are preordained to be fulfilled and established on the earth at that time. The birthing and establishing of the Church was one of those special times. The apostle Paul experienced such an appointed time for the mystery of the Church to be revealed. "By revelation He made known to me the mystery . . . which in other ages was not made known to the sons of men, as it has now been revealed by the Spirit to His holy apostles and prophets" (Ephesians 3:3–4). Paul declared that God made him a minister of the Church:

> To make all see what is the fellowship of the mystery, which from the beginning of the ages has been hidden in God who created all things through Jesus Christ; to the intent that now the manifold wisdom of God might be made known by the church to the principalities and powers in the heavenly places, according to the eternal purpose which He accomplished in Christ Jesus our Lord.
>
> Ephesians 3:9–11

A Predestined Time for Further Revelation

The restoration movement of the 1950s was the time God chose to reveal to His holy prophets and apostles that all of the revivals, awakenings and Holy Spirit outpourings of the Second Reformation were not just random acts of God but were predestined and planned restoration movements that would fulfill God's purpose for His Church. I was birthed into that restoration reality in 1952 and received the revelation of God's progressive restoration of the Church. Twenty years later He gave the anointing and revelation to perceive future moves of God.

Martin Luther had no idea that he was being the instrument of God to launch heaven's decree to begin the great period of Church restoration, the Second Reformation (see Acts 3:21). None of the restoration reformers of the following restoration movements had any idea they were being instrumental in launching a restoration movement of the Holy Spirit. After the Protestant movement in the 1500s came the evangelical movement in the 1600s, the holiness movement in the 1700s, the divine healing movement in 1880 and the Pentecostal movement in 1906. The progressive nature of the restoration was not made known until the restoration movement of 1948 that went around the world in the 1950s. That is when revelation came that these times of refreshing were not just independent revivals that came every so often to revive the Church and keep it alive until the Rapture took all the saints to heaven. The pastors of these past revivals had no insight that they were restoration movements that would restore truth and ministries back into the Church that had been lost during the dark age of the Church. They were deliberately activated by the Holy Spirit, who was commissioned by Jesus Christ to restore certain truths and ministries at that time.

Like the Temple in Jerusalem being rebuilt in the days of Ezra and Nehemiah, the Protestant reformers cleared all the dead works off the foundation of the Temple so that the whole building could be rebuilt and fully restored. The foundational doctrine of repentance from dead works was laid, and all the following movements were built on that foundation (see Hebrews 6:1). Jesus was reactivating His decree that He would build His Church, and He is still in the process of perfecting it. For Jesus cannot return for His Church until Ephesians 4:11–15, Hebrews 10:13, Acts 3:21 and other Scriptures are fulfilled.

I received the revelation that heaven had decreed the beginning of the third and final Church Reformation in 2008. I echoed that decree to the Church world and then wrote a book presenting what was being restored and God's purpose to be accomplished in His predestined time for the last Church Reformation, which would fulfill all things that the prophets have prophesied.

When I was birthed into this movement in 1952, more than 65 years ago, God birthed the revelation of Church restoration into my spirit. (If you do not have a good understanding of the restoration movements, they are described in detail in my book *The Eternal Church*.) I did twenty years' research into everything I could find covering every revival, refreshing and movement that had taken place in Church history before I wrote on the origination, deterioration, restoration and destination of the Church in *The Eternal Church*. Nearly half that book covered the restoration movements of the last half millennium. (October 31, 2017, marked exactly five hundred years of Church restoration.) In 1955 I started teaching a series on the restoration of the Church in the local church where I was pastoring; in 1981, after three years of writing, *The Eternal Church*, my first book, was published.

Proclaiming Future Movements

In *The Eternal Church* a prediction was made that there would have to be a Holy Spirit movement to restore Christ's ministry of apostle and prophet back into the Church.* God made a decree in 1987 that it was the season for the prophets to be restored to active ministry in the Body of Christ with acceptance and recognition that pastors, evangelists and teachers have had for centuries. I thought it would be good to let this be an example of how a modern-day divine decree is fulfilled after it is made. The following is an excerpt from *Prophets and the Prophetic Movement*.†

Prophetic Labor Pains: We were pregnant with this ministry for quite some time. When a woman is pregnant with a baby, she carries it nine months, but when a man or woman of God becomes pregnant with a vision that is destined to become a restoration movement in the Church, they carry it for years. Labor pains can begin one year without the birth taking place till a year later.

Our beginning labor pains came at Christian International's (CI's) first International Prophets Conference near Destin, Florida. As far as I can determine by historical research, it was the first National Prophets Conference ever conducted in the history of the Church. More than 700 attended this gathering. On Friday, October 23, 1987—the third night of the conference—God moved in a sovereign sweep of His Spirit at 10:00 in the evening. A spirit of intercessory warfare prayer and praise arose spontaneously within all the people, and for the next 45 minutes there was a heavenly warfare in the Spirit like few have ever witnessed.

Visions and prophecies were given by many of those present, revealing what had just transpired. The main emphasis of the words given was that the battle had been won for the release and activation of the great company of prophets that

---

* The history of the prophetic movement is recorded in the second book of my trilogy on the prophetic: *Prophets and Personal Prophecy*, *Prophets and the Prophetic Movement* and *Prophets, Pitfalls and Principles* (Destiny Image, 2001).

† Hamon, *Prophets and the Prophetic Movement*, 94–96.

God had preordained to be raised up in this century and even at this very time. The sovereign move of God in the service was the preliminary labor pain that placed the baby prophetic movement in proper position along the birth canal for delivery the following year.

The Birth of the Prophetic Movement: One year later, the second CI International Prophets Conference was meeting in the ballroom of the Sandestin Beach Resort Inn in Sandestin, Florida, just 15 miles west of the CI campus. It was October 15, 1988, the third night of the conference. At 10:15 PM, when I had finished preaching on God's purpose for His great company of prophets being brought forth, a spirit of travail arose within me, and a mighty anointing swept over me as I began to travail in spiritual birth. The same spirit swept throughout the audience of more than 800, and for the next 50 minutes most of us travailed in prophetic intercessory prayer.

This intensified in my spirit until I felt my soul was being torn out as we cried out in the travail of birth pangs. I almost physically passed out from the intensity of the anointing and spiritual birth pangs. Finally, my whole body felt "weak as water," as if my very life was going out of me. I crumbled onto my knees and was immediately caught up in the Spirit. Then I saw a vision of God lifting me and many others to a higher realm. He gave me a vision of the thousands of prophets He was bringing forth at this time.

A New Baby: This company of prophets was in the hand of God like a baby which had just been brought forth from the womb. He asked if I would take a fathering role in helping Him raise up to maturity this new baby He had birthed. He stated that a new anointing and authority had been granted for this purpose and that all who were there and those around the world who received His vision for the company of prophets would receive that same anointing.

As I ascended with Jesus in the Spirit, all those present ascended also and began to form into a network structure that would propagate the prophetic. I looked and saw other networks arising all over the world. He said this was the network He had given me and that the others were several prophetic groups that He would raise up. I was to work to help bring unity, relationship and networking among the different camps of prophets.

Christ's Company of Prophets: God revealed other things that night as well about His purpose for prophets. But what I want to emphasize here is that those present sensed the revelational reality that an *official decree* had been given in heaven for the activation and proclamation of Christ's company of prophets. Some of these prophets had been in progressive preparation for many years; others had been hidden away in the wilderness like the prophet Moses. Many prophets were just now coming forth.

This company would now begin to be manifest upon the earth. They were to lead God's people out of religious bondage and give prophetic proclamations to national leaders and systems, saying, "Let God's people go!"

The Prophetic Blastoff: The "launching pad" of preparation and the "space shuttle" of the prophetic movement had been in a state of preparation for years for God's appointed time for launching. The countdown had begun several years before and finally progressed to the moment of blastoff.

Time and History Will Tell: Being a Church historian, I know that only time and history can determine the factual reality of a prophetic revelation and declaration. I am thoroughly convinced by God's divine visitation and all that I received from Christ that October 15, 1988, was the launching of the prophetic for CI and the Church world into a prophetic movement. That night I surrendered unconditionally to Christ Jesus as I received the commission from Him to take a fathering responsible role in God's purpose for His company of prophets, which are to personify Christ Jesus and to perpetuate His divine purpose for His Church on planet earth.

Only time and history will reveal whether one of the seven divine Church restoration principles was at work that night, which is, "Someone at some insignificant place must be used to launch what God wants activated." I personally believe that God's timely purpose for His prophets was officially birthed into the Church world on October 15, 1988, and was launched into what has become known in the 1990s as the prophetic movement. It was a successful launching, and the prophetic movement is now orbiting around God's eternal purpose for His Church and for planet earth. God has purposed that the prophets will continue growing in number, maturity and power until they fulfill their purpose of "making ready a people" and "preparing the way" for the return of Christ as King of kings and Lord of lords (Luke 1:17; Isaiah 40:3–5).

My book *Apostles, Prophets and the Coming Moves of God* was published in 1997. It thoroughly covered the ministry of the apostle and the prophet and how they relate to the rest of the Body of Christ. This book gives the most complete coverage of the apostle and the other fivefold ministers. In the last four chapters, I project what the next three moves of God will be. I knew that when all fivefold ministers were fully restored and fulfilling their commission of equipping the saints, a saints movement would emerge. When the saints were all trained and activated, then God could make them soldiers in His army and thereby activate the army of the Lord movement. Then the last Holy Spirit movement would fulfill the prophetic Scripture in Revelation 11:15 that the kingdoms of this world are to become the Kingdom of our Lord Jesus and His Church. For that reason I call it the Kingdom-establishing movement.

Birthing the Apostolic at CI

The apostolic for CI was birthed in 1998 at CI's International Gathering of Apostles and Prophets, which has been conducted

196

every October for the last 32 years. Apostle Dutch Sheets ministered Wednesday night on the Father's heart. At the end of his message he asked me to come forward and release Father God's heart to all the ministers and saints that were there. I prayed an impartation prayer for about five minutes, and then I had a vision of a flaming heart about the size of a basketball coming straight at me. It was placed right into my chest. It knocked me to the floor, and I went immediately into prophetic intercessory birthing prayer. While I and several who came up to pray for me were praying, Dutch was walking back and forth on the platform declaring over and over that the apostolic was being birthed!

I had been declaring for years that when all fivefold ministers were restored and actively fulfilling their commission of activating and equipping the saints, there would be a birthing of the saints movement. In 2007 at our Prophetic Watchmen Conference there was a mighty move of the Holy Spirit, and everyone there witnessed that the saints movement had been birthed. Cindy Jacobs first declared it, and it was met with agreement by everyone there.*

Then, in the spring of 2008, God revealed to me that heaven had decreed that the third and final Church Reformation had been birthed into the Church. The saints movement had activated the Third Reformation just as the Protestant movement had activated the Second Reformation and just as the John the Baptist movement had prepared the way for the First Reformation. (I talk more about this in *Prophetic Scriptures Yet to Be Fulfilled*, which focuses on revealing God's purpose for the Third Reformation.)

---

* Among those giving their agreement were Dutch Sheets, Chuck Pierce, Lou Engle and Barbara Yoder. Numerous CI ministers were also ministering alongside me: Apostles Tom and Jane Hamon, Dr. Tim Hamon, Apostle Leon Walters, Prophet Jim Stevens, Bill Lackie, Gale and Shelly Sheehan and many others.

In 2015, God revealed another part of the Third Reformation that needed to be made known. This Reformation was bringing revelation and ministry to make the Kingdom of God known, demonstrated and established in the earth. This we already understood. But now God was declaring His World War III. The advancing Kingdom would be like the U.S. Army and Navy, which operate on earth. But in God's World War III, His Air Force would clear the heavenlies, shoot down strongholds and establish no-fly zones over areas, thus clearing the powers of darkness and the devil's hosts out of the atmosphere.

God's Timing and Purpose for Divine Decrees

Every decree that heaven authorizes has a time and purpose: "To everything there is a season, a *time* for every *purpose* under heaven . . . a time there for every purpose and for every work" (Ecclesiastes 3:1, 17). God is looking for those who will sound forth God's *decrees* and *purposes* to be fulfilled at the Father's appointed times (see Galatians 4:2).

All of God's decrees are revealed from heaven to a man or woman on earth. God in heaven does nothing on earth without first revealing His timing and purpose to His prophets (see Amos 3:7). We are not talking about decrees that individuals make for their own needs and vision but those that affect Christ's Church and His purposes for mankind and earth.

A Decree and the Power for Fulfillment

On October 4, 1995, a hurricane named Opal was headed straight toward the western part of the Panhandle of Florida. It was a category 4 hurricane as it headed straight toward our CI campus in Santa Rosa Beach. We had 24 acres on the north side of Highway 98 filled with trailer homes and administrative

offices. The 40 acres on the south side held the church building and several trailer homes. Through intercession we had
redirected several storms that at one point were headed toward
us, but Opal was coming on fast and furious. The sheriff's
department had ordered everyone in South Walton County to
evacuate. My wife and I decided not to evacuate but to stay and
war for the preservation of our campus. We decreed that our
property would be preserved and that no homes or buildings
would be damaged. We moved into the church with a couple
of other families, and all that night we walked back and forth
throughout the church, praying forcefully in tongues, especially
during the height of the storm. When daylight came, we examined the area. Not one of the trailer homes had even a tree
fall on them. Trees fell to the right and left of the trailer homes
and ministry buildings, but none fell on them. At that time my
wife and I were living in our condo on the beach. Opal brought
a fifteen-foot tidal surge. Our condo was on the top floor, but
the roof was intact and no windows had been blown out. And
yet, from Panama City to Pensacola hundreds of homes were
destroyed all along the Gulf Coast. We had to cancel our October conference and move it to the following January.

The next day the news showed a diagram of the hurricane
parting right at our condo, which is directly south of the CI
campus. There was a strip in the middle, about three miles wide,
that came right over our campus with only category 1 winds,
but on either side of this strip, to the east and to the west, were
category 3 winds.

We made the decree and then prayed in tongues all night, producing the power that helped fulfill the decree, which activated
angels to war on our behalf. What the devil meant for evil, God
worked together for our good. Up to that time the highest number
that had attended our October conference was five hundred. In
January 1996, however, we had around seven hundred, and it has
not dropped below that number since that time; we have steadily

had between seven hundred and twelve hundred attendees. Dare to make decrees and follow them through to their fulfillment!

The Power of Words

Jesus, Commander in Chief of His army of saints and angels, is called the Word of God. Out of His mouth comes a sharp sword (the Word of God) with which He can strike the nations (see Revelation 19:13–15). Jesus Himself shall rule the nations with a rod of iron, which is the Word sword. His overcomers are given the same authority to rule the nations with that same rod of iron (see Revelation 2:26–27).

The greatest offensive weapon the Christian warrior has is the Word of God in his or her mouth, spoken with wisdom and authority. It is the sword Jesus used to defeat the devil in His first major battle in the wilderness. We are told to take up "the sword of the Spirit, which is the word of God" (Ephesians 6:17). Learn to wield it to do damage to the enemy of our souls. These Scriptures will help you:

> For the *word of God* is living and powerful, and sharper than any *two-edged sword*.
>
> Hebrews 4:12

> In the beginning was the Word, and the Word was with God, and the Word was God. He was in the beginning with God. All things were made through Him, and without Him nothing was made that was made.
>
> John 1:1–3

Everything in Heaven and earth, visible and invisible, was made by the word of God spoken from the mouth of eternal God.

"The *words* that I [Jesus] *speak* to you are spirit, and they are life."

John 6:63

Death and life are in the *power of the tongue.*

Proverbs 18:21

It is by the power of the tongue that we speak words. Words can create life or death and speak life and death to mankind and to the natural world.

If anyone does not stumble in *word*, he is a perfect man, able also to bridle the whole body.

James 3:2

The tongue can set things on fire with the words that it speaks. It can defile or sanctify the entire body speaking only words.

Let God [the Word] be true but every man a liar [any thought, word, action or circumstance that is contrary to God's word] ... "that You may be justified in Your *words*, and may *overcome* when You are judged."

Romans 3:4

Out of the abundance of the heart the *mouth speaks.* . . . For by your *words* you will be *justified*, and by your *words* you will be *condemned.*

Matthew 12:34, 37

Be *doers* of the *word*, and not hearers only, deceiving yourselves.

James 1:22

If a person keeps hearing the word of truth without believing, receiving and acting on it, that person opens himself or herself up to a spirit of deception.

"Do not fear, Daniel, for from the first day that you set your heart to understand, and to humble yourself before your God, *your words* were heard; *and I have come because of your words.*"

Daniel 10:12

"Is not My *word* like a *fire*?" says the LORD, "and like a *hammer* that breaks the rock in pieces?"

Jeremiah 23:29

"I will *make My words in your mouth fire*, and this people wood, and it shall devour them."

Jeremiah 5:14

So said the Lord of Hosts to Jeremiah because the people-pleasing prophets were prophesying words that did not come from God in order to contradict what Jeremiah was prophesying.

I *prophesied* [the word of the Lord] as I was commanded; and as I prophesied, there was a noise, and suddenly a rattling; and the bones came together, bone to bone. Indeed, as I looked, the sinews and the flesh came upon them. . . . [Again] I *prophesied* as He commanded me, and breath came into them, and *they lived*, and stood upon their feet, an *exceedingly great army.*

Ezekiel 37:7–10

In 2014 God revealed that the prophetic movement had entered the second phase of its purpose and prophetic ministry. The last 27 years have been the noising abroad of the message, with prophets coming alive and active from the valley of dry bones and then coming together in networks, causing a great body of prophets to appear around the world. But since 2014 we have entered the first of three phases of the fifth doctrine of Christ: resurrection of the dead, which is resurrection life. The prophets are to prophesy resurrection life to the Church until the saints come alive and stand upon their feet to become an *exceedingly great army*, God's World War III warriors.

ENLIGHTENMENT, DECLARATION AND PRAYER

Lord Jesus, Your Word reveals that our main weapon of war is Your Word in our mouths, spoken, shouted and decreed. From God's creation to all that the Bible speaks of being accomplished, everything was by the spoken decrees of God personally and through His prophets. Jesus, I want to accomplish Your purpose through my life by declaring Your Word and making decrees. I will continually fill my heart and mind with Your Word so that I can do the works that You did. Your Word and Your name have power over everything in heaven and earth and the whole universe.

12

Soldier Saints

Though every Christian is called to serve in God's army, not every saint is called to the same function. Like any army, the army of the Lord requires a variety of people with different skills to sustain itself. It has three main divisions: preaching, praying and provision.

Preaching

Saints called to preach include all fivefold ministers, missionaries and those working in full-time ministry, preaching, counseling and delivering saints from the work of Satan. They are the ones who pull people out of the kingdom of darkness into God's Kingdom of light. They are what we refer to as full-time ministers, working both within the local church and itinerantly.

Ministers called to preach have the same commission that Jesus gave those He chose to be His representatives:

He gave them power over unclean spirits, to cast them out, and to heal all kinds of sickness and all kinds of disease. . . . "As you go, preach, saying, 'The kingdom of heaven is at hand.' Heal the sick, cleanse the lepers, raise the dead, cast out demons. Freely you have received, freely give."

Matthew 10:1, 7–8

I charge you therefore before God and the Lord Jesus Christ, who will judge the living and the dead at His appearing and his kingdom: *Preach the word!* Be ready in season and out of season. Convince, rebuke, exhort, with all longsuffering and teaching.

2 Timothy 4:1–2

They do the works that Jesus did in destroying the works of the devil, presenting Jesus as the Way to be, the Truth to believe and the Life to live. Jesus was filled with the Holy Spirit and power and went about doing good and healing all who were sick and oppressed by the devil (see Acts 10:38). The warriors in God's World War III will demonstrate all that Jesus empowered and commissioned His disciples to do.

Praying

Praying saints are the faithful Christian soldiers who intercede in prayer for the frontline warriors. They are just as vital as the warriors shooting the guns, flying the planes that drop bombs on the enemy and driving the tanks that destroy the enemies of Christ's Church and His Kingdom. The praying saints have to win the battles in prophetic intercessory prayer before the battles can be properly won on the battlefield. Warriors in the army of the Lord do not fight with natural weapons against a natural enemy; they fight a spiritual war against the spirit forces of hell.

When I am traveling in ministry in other nations, I can tell the difference when my prophetic prayer warriors are praying for me back home. I am sustained and empowered; it is as if I am surrounded by a force field of God's presence. When they are not praying and interceding for me, I get easily tired, and both traveling and times of ministry do not go as well. Anyone who is going to minister in warfare definitely needs strong, prophetic intercessory prayer warriors praying for him or her. The reason I say prophetic prayer warriors is because they receive words of knowledge about situations I am facing, and they receive discernment concerning spirit forces that I am encountering out on the front line of the battlefield. By the Spirit, they take control of contrary situations and bind demonic forces that are seeking to come against the ministry. There is no separation of distance or time in prayer, because the prayer warriors are with me in spirit, battling unto victory.

In God's World War III, the Church desperately needs His prayer division increased and activated into new weapons, which are mainly the gifts of the Spirit. The Holy Spirit gifts are to be activated in the prayer division of the army just as they are supposed to be actively working in the preaching division. The term *prayer warriors* is not just a saying; they really are active warriors. Many saints are being called and activated into prophetic warfare to fight for the fulfillment and glorious victory of God's World War III.

Provision

Every army needs provision while on the field. Those who are in the provision division of the army are responsible for helping provide all the natural resources that are needed to accomplish God's purpose. The biggest portion of this would be finances that provide for the headquarters and means of travel to convey warriors to places of battle.

In a natural army, this division would include the companies and workers that produce the ships, aircraft carriers, planes, tanks, guns, ammunition and trucks and those who transport the food and water for the warriors' bodies and ammunition for their guns. It takes twelve military personnel to support one soldier on the front line. But it takes hundreds of civilian companies and thousands of civilian workers to produce all that the military needs to fulfill its purpose: protecting the citizens and making war against those who seek to destroy its nation.

The seven-mountain saints fit in this division. They are also equipped to fulfill some aspects of the other two divisions of God's army. They are to be kingdom influencers and declare the Kingdom of God to their mountain of influence. They are to pray prophetically and receive the mind of Christ so that they can be greater demonstrators of the Kingdom. All that is available to the preaching and praying divisions is also available to the provision division in God's World War III.

To summarize:

The preaching division is to teach, impart, train, activate and equip the provision division in spiritual knowledge, wisdom and warfare.

The provision saints are to share their wisdom, experience and financial resources with the preaching division.

The praying division is to pray for the other two, and the other two are to impart to the praying division.

One night, after I had preached a message challenging everyone to become mighty warriors for Jesus and His army, the Lord spoke to me, saying that I was trying to make every Christian a frontline soldier. He reminded me that in a nation of citizens, a small percentage are in the military, and in the military not everyone is a frontline soldier. Some are cooks, truck drivers who drive supplies to the front lines, office workers or in many other military positions that do not require frontline warfare. He said I should preach and challenge the saints to be soldiers in God's army but not try to make them all frontline fighters. Every child of God is called to be a soldier in the army of the Lord, but not everyone is called to fight the enemy on the front line of battle. Nevertheless, every soldier must go through basic training, submit to the rules and regulations of that nation's army and wear the uniform of the soldier.

Every Christian needs to be trained in the fundamentals of the faith and wear the uniform, or, as the apostle Paul describes it, our warrior armor. We need to be clothed with the robe of righteousness and garment of praise. We must go through boot camp to be in good shape physically, so that we are able to run the race and fight the good fight of faith. We must know our weapons and how to use them in warfare. All Christians need to exercise themselves in spiritual knowledge and ministry and be educated and activated in the special grace and gifts they have been given. The Bible declares that every Christian has received divine ability to manifest one or more of the gifts of the Holy Spirit in order to bless the Body of Christ and do spiritual warfare (see 1 Corinthians 12:7).

Every Christian may not be called to lead in spiritual corporate warfare on the front line of battle, but every Christian must know how to overcome and gain victory over the world, the flesh and the devil. Your pastor or your family cannot fight all your battles for you. Many books have been written to teach Christians how to do personal spiritual warfare to protect against the powers of darkness, but in this book, I have taught the Church how to do corporate aggressive, offensive spiritual warfare. It was written to be one of the instruments used by the Holy Spirit to help Christ Jesus raise up enough soldiers to co-labor with Him as mighty warriors in His army and to fulfill and win God's World War III.

Every Soldier Working to Win

The United States declared war in 1941 shortly after Pearl Harbor was bombed. Men signed up voluntarily to fight against those who had declared by their actions that they were out to destroy us. Immediately, manufacturing was accelerated to produce all the weapons that would be needed to fight strategically and to successfully win the war. Every military person and civilian was conscious of the war effort. And, for the most part, everything men and women worked toward was with the war in mind. My father-in-law and his brothers were sheep shearers. They were exempt from the draft and training as frontline warriors because what they were doing contributed to the needs of the war. They felt as though they were soldiers in the war because they were doing that which would contribute to the success of the war.

This is what I am trying to convey. Every present-day saint should be knowledgeable that we are in World War III, fighting against enemies that are determined to destroy us. Whatever division of the army of the Lord you are in, you need to be working with the same goal in mind: helping to win the war. You need to know that you are a soldier in God's army. This is very different from a flesh-and-bone army or a special forces unit like the Army Green Berets or Navy SEALs. God wants every saint to be conscious that he or she is a soldier regardless of that person's position in life or work. You are a soldier in one of the three divisions of God's army. Jesus is depending on each of us to know our division, faithfully fulfill our part and co-labor with Jesus Christ, our Commander in Chief, to win God's World War III.

Break Covenant with Satan

There is one more thing Christians must do to be effective warriors in the army of the Lord: Break your covenant with the devil. When I challenge Christians to do this, they always say, "I have not made a covenant with the devil!" I then explain that I am not talking about a consciously made verbal covenant but an unspoken covenant in thinking and attitude toward the devil. *If I do not bother the devil, he will not bother me. If I don't cast his demons out of people, then he won't bother my children. If I don't give to the Church, then he won't bother my finances. If I don't make the devil angry, then he won't be angry with me. If I don't do warfare against his kingdom, then he won't bother my kingdom of job, home, marriage and children.*

You probably do not want to hear this, but if you love Jesus and are glorifying Him as Lord of heaven and earth, then the devil hates you with a passion. So quit worrying about making the devil upset. Nothing you can do can cause the devil to do right by you. Jesus said the devil is so deceived and so evil that he only comes to you to steal, kill and destroy everything that is good in your life. The devil wants to make a peace treaty with you to deceive you, disarm you and then enslave or destroy you. Satan is an enemy of Jesus Christ, and he hates anyone who loves and honors Jesus Christ. The only time the devil does not bother a church member is when that person is lukewarm, murmuring and complaining more than speaking faith and thankfulness. The devil knows he already has such a one, for he knows Jesus is going to vomit out of His mouth any Christian who is lukewarm—you have to be *in* Christ for Him to vomit you *out*—and God puts murmuring and complaining in the same sinfulness category as idolatry and sexual immorality (see Revelation 3:16; 1 Corinthians 10:6–10).

In this age of peril and terror, our only safe place is in the center of God's will, fully awake and alert to the plans of the enemy and ready to attack him any time he approaches us. The Christian's best defense is to go on the offense with a company of warriors who not only know how to defend themselves against all the wiles of the devil but also know how to destroy the works of the devil. We need to be so full of the Spirit and on fire for God that the demons cannot get close to us. I want to be so dead to self, so alive to God, so fierce against the enemy, that no demon will want to be assigned to me because I destroy every evil force that tries to come against me and God. We must have the same attitude and boldness of David when he faced the giant, Goliath.

Too many Christians think of Jesus as the God of light and goodness and Satan as the god of darkness and evil. There are not two gods. There is only one God: "I am the LORD, and there is no other; there is no God besides Me" (Isaiah 45:5). Jehovah/Jesus is the one and only true God. The devil is not now nor has he ever been a god. He has appointed himself the god of this evil world system of sin, wickedness and ungodly people. Satan is only a fallen creation of God who was, at one time, in a rulership position in God's Kingdom. His angelic name was Lucifer, and he was the worship and music director of God's heavenly universe. He was never like God, who is omnipresent (everywhere present at the same time), omnipotent (unlimited and unrestricted in His power and authority) and omniscient (all-knowing, seeing and understanding everything everywhere). Satan is limited in all those areas. In fact, the book of Job reveals that even Satan has to give account to God (Job 1:6–12; 2:1–7).

Lucifer developed pride that caused him to be deceived by believing he could overthrow almighty God and sit on His throne. He was cast out of heaven with one third of the angels, who sinned with him. All light and truth was taken from them, and Lucifer deteriorated into the evil devil and his angels into demonic spirit beings. Their realm is a kingdom of darkness that is doomed for defeat.

Greater Than the Devil

The first man, Adam, was made greater than the devil, for man was created in God's own image and likeness. The devil was a created angelic being. Now, we have been born of the Holy Spirit and filled with the Spirit and have within us the Christ who created all things, by whom all things exist. And now He lives in us. That is the reason the Word of God declares, "Greater is He who is in you than he who is in the world" (1 John 4:4 NASB). You might as well go ahead and join the army of the Lord and become a devil destroyer. No longer be neutral and passive on your leisure cruise ship, but get on your battleship, get to your guns and blow the devil out of the waters of your life, family and ministry. The best way to win today's battles, gain victories and fulfill your calling and destiny is to have a passionate love for Jesus, hate evil and become the devil's greatest enemy. Become a warrior in God's World War III!

ENLIGHTENMENT, DECLARATION AND PRAYER

Every child of God is called to be in the army of the Lord, but all do not serve on the front line. I believe my main calling is the _____ (preaching, praying or provision) division. All divisions are necessary for the army to be victorious. Jesus, help me to accept my calling and do my part to make Your army successful and fulfill God's purpose for His World War III. I am committed, as all soldiers are, to giving my life for my nation, the Church. I have reached the third level of the overcomer; I have been overcoming by the blood of the Lamb and the word of my testimony, and now I will succeed and overcome all by loving not my life even unto death. I will be a faithful warrior of God's World War III by using my God-given weapons of war and keeping on my whole warrior armor. Amen and Amen.

"Those who are with [King Jesus] are called, chosen, and faithful" (Revelation 17:14). "And they overcome [the devil and all their enemies] by the blood of the Lamb and by the word of their testimony, and they did not love their lives to the death" (Revelation 12:11).

Index

When God calls a man or woman to be a prophet, destined to have a major impact upon the Church, the calling brings with it much preparation, learning, experience and great tests. In 1950, fifteen-year-old **Bill Hamon** was living on his parents' farm with his father, mother, two brothers and two sisters, none of whom were churchgoing people. In July of that year, Bill attended a three-week revival at a brush arbor meeting about two miles from his house. Riding his horse to the meetings every night, he went to the altar on his sixteenth birthday and received Jesus Christ as his Savior. He was filled with the Holy Spirit and prayed for 45 minutes in his Spirit language. (The complete story is told in the preface of his book *Prophets and Personal Prophecy*, written by his wife, Evelyn Yvonne Hamon. It is also in his book *The Day of the Saints*.)

Over the next thirty years, Bishop Hamon was trained through attending Bible college, pastoring, evangelism, teaching at a Bible college and then establishing Christian International School of Theology. In his second thirty-plus years, he has built the Christian International Ministry Network, which now has an apostolic network of more than five thousand ministers. Recognized as the father of the modern prophetic movement, Bishop Hamon has pioneered and grown in prophetic ministry, personally prophesying to more than fifty thousand individuals, ranging from presidents of nations to babies in their mothers' arms. At the same time, he has endured major tests that were heartbreaking, mind-blowing and world-shaking, yet also part of the making of a major restoration prophet. "It takes years to develop the ten M's (manhood, ministry, message, maturity, marriage, methods, manners, money, morality and motives) that are essential to developing in and maintaining ministry," Bishop Hamon says. "It is good to desire to do great things for God; you must, however, understand that the greater the calling, the greater the testing and purifying. I fully agree with apostle Paul's declaration in Romans 8:18 (KJV): 'For I reckon that the sufferings [tests and trials] of this present time are not worthy to be compared with the glory [co-laboring with Christ] which shall be revealed in [and through] us. Press on and you shall reap in due season if you do not give up. Amen.'"

At age 21, while pastoring a church, Bishop Hamon married his wife, Evelyn. They have three children (Tim, Tom and Sherilyn), eleven grandchildren, and, as of this writing, seventeen great-grandchildren. All three of Bishop Hamon's children are ordained ministers serving in leadership roles at Christian International.

Christian International

Christian International Apostolic Network (CIAN) and Christian International Global Network (CIGN)

CIAN is a network of more than five thousand churches and ministers around the world with an apostolic/prophetic mandate to restore the fivefold ministry to the Body of Christ and equip the saints for the work of ministry.

Christian International School of Theology (CIST)

CIST offers quality biblical education through a systematic, off-campus study program, from the fundamentals of faith to present-truth prophetic and apostolic ministry. "Be established in the present truth" (2 Peter 1:12 KJV).

Christian International Equipping Network (CIEN)

CIEN provides resources, relationship and networking to apostolic and prophetic training centers around the world. From degree programs to outreach programs, CIEN supports a wide range of people and organizations who are equipping others in their gifts and purpose.

7 Mountain Kingdom Influencers (7MKI)

The 7 Mountain Kingdom Influencers program is the newest network in Christian International, equipping those called to the marketplace in their spiritual gifts and personal anointing to fulfill their destiny. Dr. Bill Hamon says that those who work in the marketplace need the same anointing, commissioning, equipping and support as those called to work within the Church.

Manual for Ministering Spiritual Gifts

More than three hundred thousand people have been trained to use the gifts of the Holy Spirit through this anointed teaching. This seminar combines sound biblical truth with Christian International's proprietary role of activating others. "Be doers of the word, and not hearers only" (James 1:22).

Annual International Gathering of Apostles and Prophets (IGAP)

More than thirty years ago, CI called the first international gathering of apostles and prophets in the Body of Christ. Each year, believers gather to receive global direction from God through His modern-day apostles and prophets. This event takes place the third week of every October, Tuesday through Friday.

Annual Watchman Intercessor Assembly

At the annual Watchman Intercessor Assembly, we do not just petition God. We listen to what He says from heaven, and we decree it, implement it and act on it. This reformation mindset has set Christian International at the forefront of entire movements that have changed the face of the Church. The Watchman Intercessor Assembly is the first and only national prophetic watchman/warfare gathering of its kind.

Ministry Training College & Leadership Training Institute

Ministry Training College (MTC) is an extension of our Equipping Network and of CI's home base church, Vision Church, in Santa Rosa Beach, Florida. MTC fulfills part of the purpose God gave CI to mature and prepare the Church, when He spoke to Dr. Bill Hamon that He "makes the man/woman before He makes the ministry." MTC's motto is "Know your God, know yourself, know your ministry and fulfill your purpose."